The Rose of September
(true stories)
by
Oksana Verpakhovskaya
ISBN: 978-1-9997646-3-0

About the author:

Oksana Vasilyevna Verpakhovskaya is a chief research scientist in the Sexopathology and Andrology Department of the "Institute of Urology at National Academy of Medical Sciences of Ukraine" obstetrician-gynecologist, Doctor of Medical Science, professor.

"After long years of working as an obstetrician-gynecologist, an opportunity to help others became part and parcel of natural human interaction for me. It is this amazing peculiarity of a medical profession that allowed me to uncover the uniqueness of human destinies and life stories. They astonish, inspire and infuse belief in the inexhaustible opportunity to maintain hope in a better future even in the hardest situations. Their value lies in the fact that they reflect the life itself, not the author's imagination…"

Eleven real stories. They amaze, inspire, and help you to believe in the inexhaustible opportunity to keep hope, even when there seems to be no way out. The theme of a doctor's role in patients' lives runs like a scarlet thread through each story writer by the author - a practicing obstetrician-gynecologist.

Aimed at non-specialist female audience.

Author biography:

Oksana Romashchenko (maiden name: Verpakhovskaya)

Doctor of Medicine; Professor; Obstetrician-Gynaecologist.

Chief Scientific Officer of Sexology and Andrology Department, State Institution 'Institute of Urology of the National Academy of Medical Sciences of Ukraine'

Vice-President of the Ukrainian Association of Sexologists and Andrologists; Member of the European Society for Sexual Medicine.

In 1989, Verpakhovskaya obtained a Candidate of Medical Sciences degree after having defended a thesis 'The Role of Chlamydia Infection in the Emergence of Female Infertility'.

In 1994, Verpakhovskaya was on a secondment in Paris, France, within the research project 'Improvement of System of Family Planning in Ukraine'.

In 1997, Verpakhovskaya received scholarship from World Health Organization and went through specialized training in Brussels, Belgium, within the program 'Diagnostics, Treatment and Preventive Maintenance of Sexually Transmitted Infections. Treatment of a Couple'.

In 2001 a Doctor of Medical Sciences degree was obtained with a thesis 'Inflammatory Diseases of

Genitals in Girls and Teenagers: Diagnostics, Treatment and Prognostication'.

Since the thesis defence in 2001, Verpakhovskaya has been working in the Department of Sexology, and Andrology of the State Institution 'Institute of Urology of the NAMS of Ukraine'.

In 2010, in cooperation with Marlena Bouche, Verpakhovskaya prepared a book for teenagers 'Questions that Are Worth Being Asked' and had printed 100 thousand copies. The book was presented in Ukraine within the program of book fair in Mystetskiy Arsenal on 30 May 2011.

In 2012 the book 'Life Anamnesis, or Stories of Love' was issued, and then in 2013 the book 'Simple Joys of Elegant Age' was published.

In 2012, Verpakhovskaya, obtained the academic title 'Professor' within specialty 'obstetrics and gynaecology'.

Verpakhovskaya is the author of 259 scientific articles and 4 scientific monographs.

Verpakhovskaya has supervised three Candidate thesis papers and one Doctoral thesis paper defended on modern tendencies of urogynaecology and female sexology.

Main scientific directions: urogynaecology, female sexology.

Table of Contents

In Lieu of a Preface, or Why I Started Writing 7

My Love is Always Here for Me   10

Coming Back to Reality   19

When She Was Crossed Out   23

A Shot of Happiness   40

Little Black… Coat   48

Snow Outside the Window   56

Smile of a Newfoundland Dog   63

Eternity   68

Smell of the Long-Gone Spring   84

The Rose of September   95

"Miracle Is Where You Are…"   102

Love is patient, love is kind. It does not envy, it does not boast, it is not proud.

It does not dishonor others, it is not self-seeking, it is not easily angered, it keeps no record of wrongs.

Love does not delight in evil but rejoices with the truth.

It always protects, always trusts, always hopes, always perseveres.

1 Cor. 13: 4-7

One evening, flipping through TV channels, I accidentally found an interview given by an editor of a fashionable magazine. It was a woman in her thirties with a flawless hair and makeup, well-groomed in the current esthetic fashion. Self-confidently enunciating her words in a metallic voice, she was pontifying, "The times of Cinderellas and mousy women have gone. Today is the time of bright women, so-called vamps, who know what they want and how to attain their goals. It's the time to be active!" From what I saw, it was obvious that she embodied these characteristics and strived to be a style icon for the world.

Alas, it is so typical of today's world to utter such statements and describe the life curve point by point, imposing one's stereotypes of success! But is it possible that all of us want to have an opportunity and desire to make one's destiny fit someone else's rigid framework of success? Spiritually blind chasers for this philosophy end up sacrificing something valuable when lying down in this bed of Procrustes, don't they? And does everyone want to be like this? Does everyone need to be like this? We're so different, after all!

Instantly I got a desire to call on this statement. I knew for sure that my wish to resist was based not on narcissism due to my own achievements. Being an obstetrician-gynecologist, I have observed thousands of destinies during the years of practice, and each of them is unique. This is the nature of a medical profession –you unwillingly become a witness of landmark moments in the lives of those who strive for help. And sometimes – not only a witness, but also a participant. But I know exactly that every Cinderella has her own chance, and behind a "mousy person" there can be an extremely interesting individual who aspires to attain happiness. After all, any person, whether they have achieved overall recognition or look at the sunrise through a foggy window, unfailingly hopes for and believes in their happiness.

After the years of work, I haven't lost my ability to wonder at unpredictability of ups and downs and have recognized their uniqueness. One doesn't have to apply for the help of a writer's fantasy, since the most fabulous and unbelievable stories are given by the life itself. This is how I started writing…

Let's leave it for literature critiques to determine the epic prose mini-form of my creative works – whether they are novels, documentals, or narrations. I hope the admirers of harlequin novels will forgive me, for even though the narration is similar (all my stories are about women) I'm not a fan of this artistic genre. I dare to affirm that all these stories are completely real and only names of the characters have been changed. Eleven authentic stories. They amaze, inspire and allow believing in the inexhaustible opportunity to preserve hope in the most hopeless cases. After all, faith, hope and love are the best medicine for all physical and emotional sufferings. The value of my essays is proved by the fact that they originate from the life itself, not from the author's imagination.

I dedicate this book to Alla & Vasiliy Verpakhovskiye

My Love is Always Here for Me

This is a story about a woman whom I've been friends with for many years. When I started studying at Kharkov Medical University, I needed to rent an apartment, which my mom had managed to find after great effort. I'll never forget how it felt, moving as a sixteen-year-old girl, to a large city after living such a slow-paced life. Nor will I forget how it felt when my mom left in a tram, taking my previous life with her. I had been stood on the tram crossroads for a long time, struggling to control my tears, feeling immense helplessness in a strange new world...

I moved into a shared apartment - where Unya Dmitryevna, an amazing woman with a special sense of humour - occupied two rooms. She was a chubby woman with small feet. I was stunned how her legs, wearing low-heeled shoes, could withstand such a heavy body. Unya Dmitryevna had short hair, adorned with a cutesy forelock. When I first met her, she looked at me curiously, and said, "My girl, can you even guess at what sort of a life is ahead of you? You'll be drowning in love. To be honest, we'll need to hack upon your appearance for that. But it's gonna be fine."

After a week, Unya Dmitryevna's friend had already managed to give me a facial, and a woman-next-door, Larisa (an assistant director at a cemetery)had managed to place a safari print dress onto my curves.Alongside Larisa and Unya Dmitryevna, another family lived in the apartment. Rimma Stefanovna was the head of the family. She was a plump, blonde woman, who always wore her hair up, framing her round face. with her hair up and a round face. Her big, brown, eyes weredecorated with bold, smooth wings. The dark arrows of her eyebrows always looked to be inviting,and her bright plush lips formed a gracious smile. Rimma Stefanovna was a chief accountant in one of the leading plants of Kharkov. Even in the apartment, she liked to wear high heels, and she occasionally gave her recommendations to the tenants. Her second husband, Georgy Petrovich - a geologist, a man of harsh temper, and who was frequently annoyed with Unya Dmitryevna - liked to smoke in the hallway,repeating one and the same phrase:

"Unya Dmitryevna, stop boiling your clothes - especially your underclothes - in the pot where you usually boil a chicken."

The answer was always:

"Zhorik, what's the big deal? Go learn something smart. It won't hurt you at all."

Once, I overheard Georgy Petrovich asking Unya Dmitryevna who had sent the new tenant to her. I then heard him request that she warn me about the strict adherence to all the rules of a shared household. Rules were essential for that apartment, since we only had one toilet; one common kitchen with three tables; one bathroom, where we never had hot water, and one phone. I was always slightly afraid of the tenants, especially of Georgy Petrovich, and would try to go into the kitchen when there was no one there. And, I also visited the toilet before everyone else – it seemed to me that otherwise, it would cause anger and indignation. At first, I perceived my new surroundings to be an opportunity to discover different things, and I made efforts to adapt to its many surprises.

There was a girl named Yulya living in that apartment. She was 13 and was Rimma Stefanovna's daughter from her first marriage. Yulya was a capricious, chubby teenager, with a bush of bright-red hair braided into a plait. Yulya liked to mimic Unya Dmitryevna, and at times, would tease her, to which Unya would reply, "What a naughty young lady!" Unya Dmitryevna liked to feed Yulya after she returned from school; she would save her the best goods in the fridge.

***

Yulya entered my life on the second day of my tenancy, and as it turned out, was to remain in it for a lifetime. We grew up together, despite the fact that I was a university student and she was a schoolgirl. Yulya was the first to show me the metro, and the city. We liked to ride trams;go to the park, and walk around the Sumskaya street next to where we lived. We liked to find ourselves riddles, and we would sit in a café called 'Snowflake' on the weekends, where they sold the tastiest ice-cream in the world. It all was so special to me.

Together, with Yulya, I discovered the amazing work of Tarkovsky, a filmmaker. We would watch his films, not always understanding the message in the movies, but would still feel incredibly excited. We liked Italian and French movies. We considered them an opportunity to peep into an unknown world. We both read a lot -

plunging into the depths of romantic sentiments and emotions.

When I became older and more engrossed in student life, I began to find myself becoming estranged from Yulya a little. However, after some time, our bond grew further into a trustful friendship. Years of university flew by very quickly. I was to return to my native, small town of Haysyn, and already struggled to imagine my life without Unya Dmitryevna, Rimma Stefanovna, Uncle Zhora, and Yulya. They all loved me and had become my family.

Larisa found a decent apartment in the city center a year after I moved, and during my university years, I would visit her. She would change admirers often, however, managed to bring a hint of romance into all these relationships. Larisa always knew where to find an unusual, high-quality piece of clothing, or French perfume, and, understanding my financial situation, she would lend money for my outfits, making sure I would always look decent.

***

Now, thinking about my past, I feel a burning nostalgia for the days filled with warmth, naivety, understanding, kindness, support, and help. It was the world of interesting people who didn't waste their talents, but 'lived tastefully' (as Unya Dmitryevna liked to say). I miss my darling Kharkov citizens…

The time took its toll. Work, study, marriage, family difficulties. On my wedding day, Yulya was my maid of honor and I was happy for the chance to see this beautiful, young woman, who had started working in a design bureau after graduating from university. We spent the time recalling everyone we loved, feeling sad for the good old times that had dissolved in our past.

***

Unya Dmitryevna died of a heart attack. When Uncle Zhora found her body in her room, he was crying like a baby. She had a smile set on her face forever - proving her radiance. Uncle Zhora passed away soon after experiencing complications from his diabetes.

This loss broke Aunt Rimma and she started drinking. She showed no resistance when she was told to move from her shared apartment and found herself in a one bedroomed apartment in Saltovka. Time was flying, and Perestroika began. One day, Yulya told me that Rimma Stefanovna had disappeared.

***

We never found her and the apartment was taken since it wasn't privatized. Yulya was left alone. She came to visit me on New Year's Eve once, and said that she had met a man that she had fallen in love with and had married. They lived in her apartment and were trying to get pregnant. I discovered lots of pleasant things about this man from Yulya; he liked animals a lot and, consequently, was a vet. He lived with his mother, and obviously, was a set bachelor.

Anytime Yulya visited, we would spend hours recollecting over our past, keeping our happy memories alive. We lived together for three weeks, during which, Yulya was having treatment in the clinic where I worked. We would cook dinner together; talk deep into the night; she would read books to my son, and in the evenings we would walk the streets, trying hard not to think about current politics and social issues.

After several months, I received a phone call. Yulya was screaming into the receiver and announced that she was pregnant. We were so happy! After another month, she said that her man had left her at the insistence of his mother. And in another month, I learnt that she had been made redundant. I visited her and saw how much she had changed. It looked as though time had frozen for her; she was sitting in her father's armchair, wrapped into her mother's shawl. She said to me, abruptly, "This child is, already, my whole life. He is the only one I can count on. I have to give birth to him, and raise him right."

Throughout her pregnancy, I did my best to support Yulya. Some time after the New Year, she gave birth to a redheaded baby boy, and we were both so incredibly happy to see him.

***

Yulya managed to overcome so many obstacles, and to this day, I still struggle to comprehend how. I told Yulya's story to my wealthy patients and, I must give credit to them, they were touched, and helped her financially. A good friend of mine bought her several month's worth of baby food, a baby carrier, and a handed her a decent sum of money that was enough for about six months.

Yulya named her son after her father: Stepan/Styopa. When Stepan turned one, she leased out her apartment and they left for a village, where she rented a house. Stepan had a chronic bronchitis which required him to live in optimum environments so to keep it manageable. I could see how hard it was for Yulya to adapt to her new environment, but through our exchanging of mail and phone conversations, I could see that after a while, it became easier. Despite the mundane hardships, the year she spent in the village played a positive role for her. The next fall, Yulya returned to her apartment. She had to renovate it after the renters, and it exhausted her finances and her energy. But still, she managed to put an end to her dwelling. And the life of herself and Stepan started to improve. She was trying to find a part-time job, leaving Styopa with her neighbours or friends. Another year filled with numerous difficulties flew by; illnesses, hospitals, overloads, and a continuous lack of sleep and food.

I went to visit Yulya in spring, together with my son. We decided to baptize Styopa on an unusually sunny spring day. The priest led us to a small temple where he baptised Styopa, in that moment, making me his godmother, and my twelve-year-old son – his godfather. After the ceremony, everything felt different, brighter. The birds were singing and our hearts were filled with joy and hope for a better future. Yulya turned to me and said, with tears in her eyes,

"I'm so happy I have Styopa - I am so excited to watch him grow and change before my eyes!"

***

Styopa grew to be an ailing child. In kindergarten, he began to manifest his leadership skills. His school years revealed he had a special talent in exact sciences and nature study. He liked animals a lot, especially a cat named Murchik whom he found on a wet autumn night. Stepan was especially good at cooking, and when I visited them for a couple of days - I was astounded by his ability to create culinary masterpieces from common ingredients. He would tell me many times,

"When I grow up, I'll become a restaurant owner,, and my mom and you won't have to cook or go shopping anymore. You'll live like queens!"

I was very moved by such statements, witnessing the closeness of Yulya and himself when he would cuddle his mum and say,

"Mommy, you're the best. You really are."

***

Now, Styopa is thirteen years old. The same age Yulya was when I first met her. He's independent, emotional, and open to anything new. In the classroom, he is a leader in both his studies and peer groups, and his wish to become a restaurant owner hadn't faded away. However, a recent meeting between us revealed Stepan wished to pursue a different career to allow his mother a better life.

Yulya said that when Styopa had been a little boy, he had asked about his father. She would come up with a number of excuses for his absence and was always afraid of forgetting what she had said earlier, wanting to be consistent in her lies. When Styopa turned 12, she tried to explain everything as truthfully as possible to him. He hugged her and said,

"Mummy, you're the best, the most beautiful mum. Thank you." His father never showed any interest in him, and when Yulya had left for the village she raised her child in, she had been so desperate, she decided to call him. The male voice, that once was so near and dear, answered, "These are your problems, handle them by yourself." Since then, she hadn't seen him or heard from him.

***

During these years, Yulya hadn't had any sort of romantic relationships. All of her love -all of her feelings - were devoted to Stepan. Yulya reminded me one day, "You know how happy I am to have Styopa. He's my biggest love, and is always here for me."

Coming Back to Reality

Walking through the clinic corridor, I noticed a woman sitting near my office. Her posture gave away her inner tension, and I sensed that her decision to come for a consultation wasn't easy, rather a result of agonising self-reflection. She entered my office and sat in front of me. In the way she held herself, I saw both her strong-willed personality, and her childish naivety. The expression of her grey eyes, the slight flush on her pale cheeks, and the movements of her hands were signs of anxiety. Small wrinkles near her lips served a mark of frequent tension.

The woman's name was Anna, and she decided to share her life story with me. I could see, very clearly, that it was painful for her to rake over old ashes. But, after gradually overcoming the anxiety that coupled with her memories of the past, I learnt about her difficult childhood; when her beloved father left them;how her mother - deciding to create a new family - brought a sullen man into their home, and about how he was annoyed by Anna's presence. How, at 16 years old, she experienced despair from her stepfather's molestation, unable to share this secret with anyone else. Only years later, when he was but a memory for them, Anna told her mother. It had left Anna afraid of relationships with men.

She found her escape in the form of studying history at university. At 35 years old, writing and producing a thesis; becoming more assertive; and overcoming hardships, it seemed she had left behind her teenage self. Her studies surrounded her. She began to see the colours of the world of her heroes; hear the music of a chamber orchestra; watch the elegant ladies glide across the floor in beautiful dresses. And when she returned to reality, she would feel hurt and disappointed, the colours disappearing and being replaced with dullness. The only colour that existed in her world was when she was lecturing to students about her 'dream world', the one which became more precious to her than reality.

One day, in the lecture hall, she saw a man who was older than her other students. She started to feel anxious when he was around, and this anxiety was taking her out of the illusory world she found comfort in. Every time their eyes met, something unusual would happen – her past and her present both lost their meaning, and she found herself overwhelmed with joy and fear. They became acquainted. Her anxiety started to disappear and she began to trust and feel happiness again. Gradually, she began opening up to the world around herself; fell in love with bright colors; changed her hair and began using makeup. Their walks after lectures became a tradition. She couldn't imagine her life without them anymore.

She still didn't dare to take him into her home, her place of comfort and security. Anna was waiting for the spring, and hoped like never before that something special would happen in her life - after her beloved starlings return, and trees start blossoming.

Coming to our clinic, hoping to acquire self-confidence; rid of the burden of doubts and past experiences, she was standing on the threshold of her new life, fearing to make the first step. She was filled with worries about herself. She noticed the "awkwardness" that enveloped her, and she knew of her responsibility to both herself and the man in her life. He was the first person she had managed to open up to and trust after so long.

The sincerity and the enormous level of trust this woman carried herself with, were extremely significant to me. I could understand why after all these years, she had distanced from the real world - going deeper into the past of her heroes and finding inspiration in the ideals of previous times. I could see the incredible efforts it took her to stay placed in the real world, could witness her strong desire to feel as though she was needed and desired by, and irreplaceable to this meaningful man in her life. We had many long conversations, and it seemed to me that I helped to participated in the changes that were taking place in her life. After our talks, the hold that bitter memories held over her, was gone. I wanted sincerely for this woman to face the reality in its non-cruel form.

After six months, I received a letter from Anna. She had gotten married. All her past years now seemed to have been preparation for the main event – her real happy life. After six more months, I unexpectedly reunited with Anna in a theatre. To be more exact, I recognized her amongst the crowd of people invited to the anniversary evening dedicated to Maya Plisetskaya. She was walking, arm in arm, with an attractive, calm-looking and dignified man. I could see it in his eyes that he worshipped the woman on his arm, who was carrying his child. I was incredibly happy for Anna, and was relieved to see that her soul had become filled with real, authentic and simple, human joy.

When She Was Crossed Out

Irina was already starting to leave her office when her phone rang. Since her work day had finished an hour ago, this call was unexpected. The phone was ringing persistently and she understood that someone must have needed her very much at that moment. Irina took the receiver and heard Vera.

"Ira, I feel bad. I'm in the hospital. All alone."

Vera had been worried about Irina for some time, and the phone call, coupled with the desperateness in Irina's voice was proof enough that something had happened."Which hospital, Vera? I'm coming."

It kept on raining and it was hard to even remember when the rain started. Ira sat in the back seat of the company car and, going past the familiar city blocks, observed the slanting drops of rain hitting the window and distorting the lights of street lamps and shop-windows. Only recently, she and Vera were passing by the same road, and Irina noticed that her friend - usually so cheerful, optimistic and able to decrease tension in any situation - became unusually reserved and silent. Anxiety settled in her deep, black eyes. And even the lines she used to draw on her eyes didn't look so inviting. Her dark, shinyhair was fastened into a bun on her head, a bit higher than usual. Her bright and plump lips that used to light up a smile on her face, seemed to forget how.

After years of friendship, these two women learnt the joy of genuine communication; without jealousy, misunderstanding and fear. It was a trustful relationship of two kindred souls. Each one of them understood that their relationship was nothing but a gift of this ambiguous life. Understanding each other very well, they could limit themselves to short phrases, and sometimes even gestures, to share their thoughts. Irina often repeated to herself, "What a great happiness it is to be yourself and feel that you're accepted as you are! What happiness it is to speak sincerely and to be understood!"

Today, Irina realized that something serious had happened. She had never heard this desperateness in Vera's voice before, even when her husband wanted to leave her or when her children were sick. In this tone, Irina heard her resigned despair. Irina was lucky to get to the clinic rather quickly. Above the doors of the gynecology department, she saw a dim signboard saying "Hospital Ward." She knew this door because only recently, she and Vera had visited their doctor, and friend, Svetlana Vasilyevna. 15 years had passed since the day Svetlana Vasilyevna helped deliver Irina's child in this clinic. The arrival of her youngest son brought light to her life. Svetlana Vasilyevna became not only the doctor who delivered her child, but a friend who took part in everything happening in her life.

But on the day she visited with Vera by her side, Irina heard an unexpected diagnosis and, by the expression on her face, she understood that the situation was worse than they could imagine. Many of us can't always objectively perceive events, especially if the reality comes to have an undesirable outlook. At that time, Irina was told that she would have to come back to the clinic again. And now, she opened the heavy door, welcomed by the smell of medications and damp air. Irina spotted Vera lying in a sickbed. Her beige coat, which they had bought only recently, was draped on a chair nearby. The brim of her grey chequered skirt had a blood-red color. It was hard to recognize Vera: there wasn't even a trace of her usual flush on her pale hollow cheeks; her face's features became sharper and her dark eyes seemed to be bigger than usual because of the circles round them. It seemed that everything was hard for her – to speak, to cry and even to breathe.

    In the next room, the space was filled with an old, heavy table, and an elderly woman was sat around it, her grey hair coming out from under her cap. She was writing something into a journal which wore a tattered cover. Irina knew from first glance that even a military commander would stand to attention in the presence of this hospital ward manager. "The doctor is busy and will see this woman later." It was futile to beg her, and especially argue with her. Irina realized that she had to find another solution as quickly as possible. She ran to the second floor of the clinic and, despite the yelling of the hospital ward manager, burst into the doctor's lounge.

"There is a woman bleeding out and you're sat writing some papers here?!" Irina questioned with indignation and despair in her voice. After several minutes, they were next to Vera's bedside. After a few more minutes – Vera was taken to a small operating room. Before she left, Ira hugged her friend - the one who surrounded her with positivity and support, and went in search of a public telephone; leaving behind the doctor who was now shouting orders to his team.

Irina went to the first floor, found the telephone and fumbled for a coin. It rolled to the very bottom of her purse. After several beeps of the dial tone, she began to taste a metallic taste in her mouth as she waited for Svetlana Vasilyevna to answer. When she finally did, Irina felt relieved, and began telling Svetlana about Vera. "I will come soon." After some more time, Svetlana Vasilyevna was there, and she immediately brightened up the department.

"My dear Ira, I did tell Vera to come to see me two months ago. Now calm down and pull yourself together."

Ira sat on a sofa's edge as Svetlana Vasilyevna went to enquire about Vera's situation. She was praying. In the past few days, she had been doing it more and more often, and it gave her confidence in everything that was happening around her. . Svetlana Vasilyevna came back after 30 minutes and said that they were preparing Vera for a surgery.

"Ira, everything is under control. You are better to go home. I'll call you in the morning."

Despite her efforts, Irina decided to stay. Svetlana Vasilyevna didn't bother to insist she listened to her. After all these years, she knew how devoted Ira was. This trait of her character evoked respect from Svetlana. She allowed Irina to stay in her office.

Ira went to the hospital hall.Through the window - which was framed by short, white curtains - night was approaching. 'The floor tiles are the same as my neighbours' bathroom tiles', she thought. 'And why do they have these chairs with leatherette covering connected like in a cinema?'

Irina, already entitled to use the phone on duty, called home and said that she would stay in the hospital with Vera. After a short pause, she made a second call. She had to call Vera's husband, Vasiliy, whom Ira had been trying to avoid lately. She wasn't even surprised that he wasn't with Vera at present. But she had to make sure her children were okay – Inna was a girl of 13, while Igor was only 4 years old. She was greeted by an annoyed man's voice from the receiver. Irina inhaled deeply and held her breath, expecting a hard conversation. The soul of this man, whom Vera had loved and excused for many years, was dry like sand in the desert. With a short and almost emotionless response, he said, "Irina, I'm tired. I'm sick of these endless problems. Talk to Inna."

Despite her age, Innahelped her a lot. In many ways, she resembled her mother, but she couldn't understand one thing: why she didn't react to her father's rudeness and incontinence., Vera remained silent when he was coming home late, or didn't come home at all. She didn't ask him about anything, but tried to keep the family together, and fill the house with comfort and warmth.

Recently, her mom had started getting tired often, and Inna noticed that household activities - even those that had been pleasant for her - became almost backbreaking. Her mom could be lying down on the sofa with her eyes closed for hours. Inna felt that something was wrong, but didn't know what to do.

Irina had noticed long ago that Inna inherited all the best traits from Vera: her kindness, compassion, empathy, and cleanliness. She calmed the girl down and asked her to be grown-up, and take care of her brother. Only when Ira had returned to the doctor's office, did she feel her eyelids had become as heavy as lead. Ira cuddled into a soft cashmere shawl and recalled a recent conversation she had had with Vera, where she shared her worries about her complicated relationship with her husband. Ira knew about her husband's dispassion, and his undisguised unfaithfulness. She was trying to prevent Vera from learning the hard truth, hoping that over time, Vasiliy would start appreciating the woman who lived with him. Ira didn't want to hurt Vera, even though, at heart, she knew that it was the road to nowhere.

Being her work colleague, Ira started noticing something. The new chief director began calling Vera to his office quite frequently, demanding her to provide some reports. It didn't go unnoticed to Irina that this man, with a mop of greying hair and grey eyes, changed whenever Vera was around. He would blush, and couldn't take his eyes off her. And, as it seemed, Vera didn't care about it at all. She didn't notice anything, still daydreaming about all of her responsibilities and duties. And when Irina, overcoming her friend's inattention, made an attempt to talk to Vera about the new chief - Vladimir Andreyevich - and the attention her paid to her, she didn't even want to continue the conversation. Everyone noticed the change that occurred in him whenever Vera was present. And he was a dignified man. People said that he had been living as a bachelor, protecting himself. . Colleagues had only a tiny bit of information about his personal life.It's a rare occasion to meet a man like him, and for this reason, Vladimir earned Irina's well-grounded respect from the first meeting.

Irina was deep in her thoughts. Why do we end up disappointed so often? Why don't we meet people in time? And everything that happens to us – is it edification or punishment? Or is it only a part of the path to what we really need and want? Ira recalled her grandmother's words, "Love turns life on Earth into Heaven. Real love doesn't go away. It will never turn into evil, hatred and offence. It will always remain young. It will make a person better and fill the world with bright colors. If it doesn't happen, it's not love." This current of memories took Ira to her childhood. She recalled her meeting with her then future husband; the difficulties of the first years of their life together, "I guess Grandma meant that we need to know how to preserve love…" And then, Morpheus embraced her.

Sounds of water boiling in a pot awakened Ira. As usual, Svetlana Vasilyevna was making tea after surgery. Her tired glance meant many things – the surgery was complicated, continued for several hours, and had to be done thoroughly. Vera had already been in the resuscitation department. She lost a lot of blood.

"Dear Ira, get some rest. We'll nurse Vera."

Rain was pattering onto the window and it seemed that this unpleasant weather would stay in the city for a long time. Within an hour, Irina and Svetlana Vasilyevna were going home, driving through familiar empty streets, with the sunrise coming through the twilight, damp and dim.

***

Vera regained consciousness in a resuscitation ward. Pain in the lower part of her stomach took its toll - she was dizzy and felt as if a heavy burden was hanging on her arms and legs. She gradually started to remember things : yesterday's daytime, the despair, the speed of the events, the hospital fuss, Irina and Svetlana Vasilyevna. The doctor whom she had just recalled came onto the ward. Vera realized that her state of life fully depended on this person. What did Vera do to find herself on a sickbed at 38 years of age? She had small children at home. It wasn't likely that Vasiliy would take care of them. Why did the man she loved and trusted so much, wanting to make his life better - why did he drift away from her? She was his accomplice in everything – in studies, at work, in relationships with his friends. She was always proud of him and helped him to grow as a professional. She always kept their house comfortable and hospitable, even though it wasn't very big. She liked to accept guests, grow flowers, come up with new culinary masterpieces. But her husband remained indifferent to all these things. Their relationship began to resemble the communication of two strangers who lived under one roof. Vasiliy was annoyed with everything about Vera: the way she walked, her hair, any attempt to start a conversation. They hadn't had an intimate relationship for a year. Of course, Vera understood that something serious was happening, but at heart, she still hoped for changes for the better.

She could be patient. She was patient as a girl, when her mother fell ill. Being a teenager, she did laundry for her entire family and took orders from a washhouse to make for living. She was patient when, entering university, she avoided noisy student parties and filled her life with work. She learnt to be patient with her needs and difficulties, remaining a kind, light, and radiant person. She was compassionate - she could share everything she had when it was needed. This is what brought her close to Irina. Their mutual understanding and support were tested over time.

A nurse came, changed a vessel in the dropper and made an injection. She was relieved of pain and Vera plunged into a translucent dream…

***

Rays of the autumn sun broke out and entered through the hospital ward's window. Vera was transferred to a ward on the lower floor. Svetlana Vasilyevna took care of giving her only one roommate. After making any sort movement, Vera's body felt strange, but there was an inner joy; the promise of a new beginning life acquired growing power, even though she still had to overcome the pain to get to it.

Days in the hospital, filled with droppers; bandaging, first steps, first walks along the hospital hall; first glance into her roommate's small mirror – she'd remember it all, forever. Svetlana Vasilyevna was always there, and after several days, her confidence in being able to return home grew. Irina would come every day and sit next to Vera's bed for several hours. Vera's sister came with her children. Seeing them, Vera couldn't hold her tears. She longed to go back home, to lay a clean, starched tablecloth on a table; change the bed sheets, put autumn flowers in her mother's vase; cook a tasty lunch, and gather all her family together. She longed for such a simple, happy household!

Her relatives, colleagues, and neighbors also came to visit her. The only person who didn't come, was Vasiliy. Her husband, whom she wanted to see more than anyone, didn't come. Each time Vera spoke about her upset, Irina would calm her down, inventing an excuse that it was a female department, and it would be difficult for men to visit. But still, Vera was waiting. She was trying not to think about it, but her thoughts would persistently evoke doubts, worries, and anxiety. Waking up at night once, she felt tears starting to stream down her face, breaking through her patience.Not being able to restrain herself anymore, she burst into tears. Her roommate, Raya, a young, red-headed woman - who was going to be discharged after her surgery - came to Vera in the darkness and calmed her down.

In the morning, when Vera opened her swolleneyes, Raya approached her. After time, they became closer, supporting each other in every movement towards recovery. Raya had many visitors, especially men. They came with presents and flowers and, in the days following her surgery, Raya wouldn't let herself been seen without makeup on. She quickly changed from her plain hospital gown, to a pink lacy peignoir, looking vivid and lively only four days after surgery. One could say that this woman infected Vera with positivity.

Raya sat at Vera's bed, took her hand in her's, looked on the lines on her palm, thought for a while and said,

"Vera, you will live a long and interesting life. And, what's most important, it will be filled with love. You will experience changes every woman dreams about. You will loved dearly, and your life will acquire meaning. You will recall my words when I'm already gone."

Raya calmed Vera down. In her heart, she knew that happiness was possible, despite everything.

***

A week, that resembled eternity, passed. Irina came to take Vera home. On the city streets, autumn was unwillingly giving the reigns to winter. When Vera was leaving the hospital, a rush of wind whipped her in the doors and she saw that the trees were completely naked. As naked as her soul. The children met their mother with warmth and a set table. Of course, it was Irina's doing. But not all her family were present. Vera went to her bedroom, and on her bedside table, she saw a letter addressed to her. It was neatly glued and signed by a smooth familiar handwriting. Even though she was expecting the worst, what she read made her stomach turn. "I don't need a half-woman. Why do I have to pretend that everything is fine? I want to cross the t's. I won't come back home. At least, this is honest. I've crossed you out."

She became weak in her knees. There were no tears. Only emptiness...

***

Four months passed. Vera came back to work. Her life had acquired a new rhythm and new colors. Everything was planned out: home, lessons, work, additional underworking. She had support from Irina and her children, who had to mature earlier than usual. Her house and its fuss was saving Vera. She was trying to make her children comfortable and happy, despite financial troubles. She liked to cook, decorate the table even for the most humble lunch and cook pastries, filling the home with fragrant smells of pies.

The 8_{th} March - women's day - was approaching. On its eve, Irina presented a gift to Vera - an elegant blouse from a business trip. Vera saw herself in mirror – a new and thinner woman whom seemed to be younger than she was. Flush returned to her cheeks and her kind eyes turned sad.

As usual, in a department where there were several women, men were arranging a celebration. Vera didn't pay attention to such celebrations. She only accepted she would make it home at a later time that day. When everyone was sat at the table, the door opened, and the chief director appeared atthe threshold. His height filled the entire door frame. He was holding several colorful bouquets in his hands. He gave them to the women - the bouquet with the most beautiful and fresh white roses intended for Vera. Vladimir Andreyevich sat in front of Vera. It was noticeable from his glance that he was happy he was here to communicate with her. Recently, he called her to his office several times,trying to move from a traditional conversation about plans and reconstructions to more abstract topics, he had received a dignified refusal from Vera. The more persistent his suggestions were, the more reserved was her reaction.

Many women looked at this powerful, sometimes abrupt, but very dignified man, some of them even managed to turn to intriguing methods to attract his attention, but their efforts weren't successful. All of the colleagues had long noticed the chief's interest towards Vera, and gossipers didn't hide their curiosity. Vera saw the efforts of this man. His ability to make decisions and always choose the right ones was well respected by Vera. But at heart, she understood that she wasn't ready for a relationship. She had a right to be afraid of new emotions after all the pain and despair she had overcome. She was afraid of any new pain, since the old wound was too deep. But unwillingly, she was thinking about Vladimir more and more often. This man was so confident in his office, but turned into a timid man, whose speech would become curt, in her presence.

At the evening's peak, Vera decided to leave. Vladimir Andreyevich caught her before she had the chance.

"Vera, Verochka, don't run away from me, at least not today."

March brought snow and Vera shivered. She noticed that an eyelash was shining on her fellow traveler's cheek. With her irresistible smile, Vera removed it from Vladimir's face. And then, unexpectedly even for herself, she invited him to visit her home. They sat in his car and after half an hour, reached their destination. Her daughter opened the door. Surprised, she looked at Vladimir Andreyevich.

"Good evening, dear! My name is Vladimir."

The events resembled a Christmas tale despite it being the start of spring. He came into their house with well-grounded and serious intentions: as a protector. His presence brought the family new horizons and a new life. It hadn't been a mistake. They had found each other.

"Verochka, I don't want to leave you for a second. I want to always be with you. When I first saw you, I realized right away – you're my soulmate. I understand that I sound like a child…"

She wanted to meet him halfway. She wanted to trust him with her life. She wasn't afraid of sharing the responsibility of bringing up her children with him. And after some time, Vladimir Andreyevich made her a proposal.

Before making a decision she came to Svetlana Vasilyevna. She needed to ask a complicated and ambiguous question. The question that had been torturing her all this time. The question was whether, considering her health, she had a moral right to say yes to this amazing man that had become so dear to her.

"Doctor, please tell me, are there any drawbacks for me after the surgery?"

"Verochka, what are you talking about? Everything is great."

"Svetlana Vasilyevna, I'm afraid of causing unhappiness to a man who proposed to me."

"Vera, don't refuse your happiness. Life is a gift, just accept it. You have a full right. You're young and beautiful. You have multiple merits and… only one drawback. You've started to frown too often, but a smile suits you so much."

Out of happiness, Vera couldn't regain her senses. She arrived to her favorite Khreshchatyk street, and a restaurant called "Metro", and took a table near a window. There weren't many people in there. A young man was sitting in front of her and looked at her with curiosity. Such an action was new to Vera and, with justified haste, she ordered a glass of rose champagne and a salad. Was this the beginning of her new life? Was the pain of disappointment going away? Spring was raging with multiple colors, not only outside the window, but inside of her. Warmth was spreading throughout her body, whether from the sip of champagne or from anticipation of saying yes. She found the nearest phone booth..

"Hello?"

"Vladimir, I need to see you."

***

They met on Saint Vladimir Hill, near their favorite place for walks, next to the "pavilion of kisses". He brought a bouquet of lilies-of-the-valley. It was a special evening. The freshness was especially noticeable in the rays of the setting sun. Vera's eyes were shining. She braced herself, looked at Vladimir Andreyevich and, overcoming her fear, she uttered,

"Until recently, I wouldn't have even believed that something like this could happen to me. I'm very grateful for you. For my feelings. I'm just happy. And I'd be glad to accept your proposal, but I have a secret that I have to tell you."

He looked at her without blinking. "Not long ago I overcame a serious gynecological surgery, and I don't know what my overlook is… And how much time I have…"

Vladimir hugged Vera and whispered,

"Verochka, my dear, no matter how much time we have – it's all ours."

***

I met Vera Ivanovna when she came to me for a consultation. Becoming closer to this amazing woman, I learnt about her life. She is evidence of the fact that life can begin when there seems to be no hope at all. They lived together for 32 years. 32 years of happiness. They united his and her children into a single, big and happy family. One could always find compassion and help in their home . Vera Ivanovna said that the grief she overcame was worth the happiness Vladimir Andreyevich gave her.

Their children absorbed the love of their parents. In this love, they became personalities, and gave birth to their own children. Their grandchildren will also transfer this love to their children. And no matter what difficulties rage outside their doors, love always lives inside. Irina was always their devoted and faithful friend.

Svetlana Vasilyevna passed away only recently. Everyone who knew her, remember her with the kindest words. Raya, her roommate from the hospital, died of an oncological disease 7 months after being discharged from the in-patient department. Vasiliy died of prostate cancer several years after divorcing Vera. Vera Ivanovna and Vladimir Andreyevich were supporting him till his last days, giving him all the help he needed.

I want all desperate and disappointed people to learn this story about Vera, about faith, hope and love. Believe, and your faith shall be rewarded!

A Shot of Happiness

At work - which has become an essential part of my life - I have an assistant nurse, Victoria, who's been by my side for many years and who probably knows me and my habits better than anyone. After many years of working together, we have learnt to understand each other well, without need for discussing things that are best left censored and confidential. By virtue of our jobs, we have had to learn the multiple fates humans can encounter, and how to help people treat their illnesses; which would result in the strengthening of the family, and an improvement in the individual's happiness and wellbeing.

I've always liked that, despite the overloads, endless nursing days and early arrivals to work, Victoria would always manage to communicate affectionately with the women who would visit the clinic, wanting to understand their situations. In the years I've known her, I've never heard her speak with an annoyance in her tone, nor have I seen her criticise anyone. My assistant had an amazing trait – a somewhat childish desire to hear that a patient's story has had a happy ending. On her table, I often saw she had women's novels. If I asked her what was so interesting about these bélles-léttres - when we witness the plots of real life novels every day at work - after a short pause Victoria would answer, "It's so wonderful to soak in the happiness of these novels… It helps me to live." And, one day, we had a chance to soak in happiness in real life.

***

It was early spring. The sun would find its reflection in everything, including the mood of our patients. A woman, whom I sympathised with very much, made an appointment to see me. Marina was 36 years old, and since the day of our first meeting (it had been almost 10 years) she hadn't changed much. She was a woman of short stature. Her tastefully chosen clothes complimented her dark skin. Her hair, tightened into a knot, fell below her shoulders. She had a high, smooth forehead; beautiful, fine eyebrows; almond shaped amber eyes; a smooth nose, and bright lips. Her proud posture and measured moves proved her control, and the trail of perfume she left behind made men automatically turn their heads. When she first came to me, I didn't doubt her success as a woman. But after each appointment, learning the details of her life, I could see, clearer and clearer, that the show she put on was hiding a wounded and suffering soul.

Marina made her first appointment with me right after her divorce, because of her chronic pelvic pain. As we found out, its appearance had coincided with the psychological trauma this woman had to face when she learnt about her husband's affair with her closest friend. They had lived together for 3 years, had a daughter whom they loved, and everything seemed to be perfect in their family. As it usually happens, Marina was the last person to learn about her husband, whilst everyone around knew even the tiniest details about what was happening. Since then , she had started experiencing a pain that made her suffer so much she started taking painkillers and sedatives in large amounts, attempting to soothe or distract herself. This pain, like a saving remedy, would divert her from her mental anguish and despair, which were much more difficult to handle. After some time, looking into the causes of the issue, we managed to overcome this physical suffering; however, its outbursts, although less intense, would still occur from time to time.

Gradually, Marina got rid of her inner brokenness, but the experience left its trace. All of her mental energy was exerted on her daughter, her home, and work. She opened her own beauty salon with the help of her ex-husband and had authority as an outstanding specialist. She communicated with people in a trustful manner, avoiding to cross the line and to open up about her life. She never let anyone in. I was glad to see Marina, because this woman aroused incredible sympathy and respect in me. After discussing medical questions, I felt the necessity to talk with her about personal topics. After all, my patient's state highly depended on that. I learnt that her interests were limited to a narrow circle: her daughter's hobbies, her parents' problems, home, work and professional growth. She read a lot, started taking an interest in art and even tried to paint herself. We talked about many things, but I couldn't sense that there was a man present in her life. I allowed myself to ask a private question.

"Marina, you're such clever girl. Why don't you want to let intimate relationships into your life? They are so important for a woman like you."

"Oksana Vasilyevna, my answer is simple – I am afraid. I won't be able to handle pain like that again. I don't believe that my life could change for the better."

I knew that dissuading Marina would serve no purpose, because her conviction was so unshakable. And suddenly, I took an adventurous decision to use other tactics. Knowing that Marina hadn't had a vacation for several years, I asked Victoria to request Yelena Nikolayevna, my old patient, to come to my room. By force of circumstances, she was in the next room. We considered Yelena Nikolayevna to be our vacation organizer because she managed to get tourist vouchers at the most reasonable prices in the highest season. After several minutes, Victoria, Yelena Nikolayevna, and I were convincing Marina to get out of the vicious cycle of her everyday life. It was a union of likeminded individuals, whom simultaneously, preached the simplest recipe for happiness. Even Marina's disbelief couldn't resist this persistent pressure, and she agreed to take a trip to Egypt.

***

After a month, Victoria, smiling cunningly, told me that Marina had made an appointment for that day. When she entered my room, I saw a drastic change in her. Her deep glance had turned into a sparkling, radiant flow and her usual, measured movements - into spurts. Her entire posture screamed her desire to share the emotions overflowing from her soul. We felt and understood that something extraordinary had happened. Not hiding her curiosity, Victoria entered the room and the two of us froze with a mute question on our lips, "How was that?" Afterwards, we heard a discrete narration that resembled a fairy tale more than a real life story. When she arrived to Sharm El Sheikh, everything was normal. She was checking into a hotel after an evening flight. Nothing foreshadowed any surprises. Then, suddenly, a representative of a tourist office came to her and, giving his apologies, offered her a stay in a neighboring hotel, where she could find a more comfortable room. Marina didn't trust him, and made a call back to Kiev to Yelena Nikolayevna, to clarify everything and get her support on the offer. Late at night, she reached her room and, when she returned to take her bag that she had left behind the door, she met a man who was leaving the room opposite to her's. He helped her to bring the bag into her room and offered to accompany her for dinner.

***

In half an hour, they met in the hall. Marina was amazed how comfortable she felt with this man. They sat at a nice table, a candle was burning brightly and the service was sweet. It all resembled a fairy tale. Surprisingly, she wasn't tired after the flight, nor was there any discomfort at her sudden change of settings. She felt the shroud of her fears and problems dissolve. She wanted this man to like her. Unexpectedly, they grew close over the course of her vacation. His name was Alexander. He had come to Egypt from Vilnius the day before. He decided to take a rest break after a 6-month business trip in Zimbabwe, where he supervised the building of roads. He was medium height, stocky, and about 35 years old. He had a flush on his cheeks. Was he anxious?

Marina was looking at this man, overwhelmed with the feeling of intrigue of what could happen. Only yesterday, she wouldn't have even agreed to speak to this man, and now she sat eating dinner with him, wanting to know all about him. She wanted a taste of happiness. When they were returning to their rooms - and walking under an arch with blossoming lianas hanging from it - Marina saw the bright moon in the sky. It enchanted her even more. She suddenly recalled the day when she, as a little girl, went with her father to see a screen version of a fairy tale, where there was a similar moon. Marina stopped Alexander and said,

"It's so strange. I've got a feeling that I saw this moon in my childhood. Back then, I foresaw everything that is happening today. It's like déjà-vu. I really want this fairy tale to continue."

He hugged her tightly and uttered,

"You are a fairy tale, indeed."

They didn't part at all during the week. A couple of days before the departure, a burning pain of separation settled in her soul. It seemed that time was flying faster than usual, and she couldn't change anything. In these 7 days, Alexander had come to mean so much to her. She wanted to know everything about him, desired to see his childhood photos, learn about his habits and attachments, meet his parents. She wanted to live his life, dissolve in his world, wait for him to return from his business trips, amaze and gladden him. She wanted to become better, more meaningful, to make him proud of her. It was such a great happiness to fall asleep and awake next to him!

***

Oh these light-hearted lovers! When they are together, nothing can break them apart. And it seems that it will last forever. When she got onto the plane, she realized that she didn't take any of his contact information, except for his phone number. And, moreover, she didn't even leave any of her information for him. She looked at her mobile phone and understood that it was the only thing that could connect her with the fairy tale world.

She returned to Kiev. She missed him tremendously. This pain was almost physical. Her life turned into an endless flow of text messages and phone calls. This unsteady happiness was enough for Victoria and I to see Marina had changed. Suddenly, the calls stopped. The world became dim. Marina was exhausted and felt the pain below her stomach start approaching with a new force. At first, she wanted to take the pill she had long forgotten about, but instead, she decided to come to an appointment with me.

Victoria and I were listening to her story, justifying the events with her lack of experience in holiday romance. And suddenly, Marina burst into tears. She cried like a baby – sincerely and desperately. None of our persuasions helped. And then I heatedly blurted out,

"Fine, you talked us into it. We'll give you something for instant happiness. We do this in the rarest occasions. I warn you: you can't get it more often than once every 6 months. Its effect lasts for a month."

Victoria looked at me with unhidden amazement. I got her to one side and asked her to make a shot of sedative. After Victoria's sacramental, "It's just a shot, it won't hurt," Marina stopped crying. Her hands dropped and she just sobbed quietly. I started prescribing my recommendations to her, telling her the details of each medication, hoping to distract her with another topic. Suddenly, the unforgettable voice of Joe Dassin from Marina's cell phone interrupted our conversation. We all froze. Astonished, Marina looked at the phone number of the caller. She cried, "Alexander, where are you? Don't disappear! Don't disappear!" And then she repeated her address and home phone number three times. She looked at us and uttered, "He's coming." Smiling mysteriously ("feebly", as Victoria said later), Marina kissed Victoria and me before leaving, and forgot her prescriptions on my table.

***

Within a week, Marina left for Vilnius to see Alexander. Her daughter also moved a bit later. I see Marina sometimes. Her "feeble" smile doesn't leave her face. She doesn't need my recommendations as pain doesn't disturb her anymore. And, after some time, Victoria also asked me to make her "a shot of happiness"…

Little Black... Coat

Every single time, starting on a new topic in scientific research, it's crucial to find a team of likeminded professionals. And this time, we had to carry out an extremely significant biochemical study, without which, the understanding of pathological processes couldn't be complete. At my supervisor's insistence, we invited a scientific officer from the Biochemistry laboratory at a different institute to join our research group. It was a well disciplinedyoung woman, whose name was Mila. When I first saw her, I was amazed to find there was a certain discrepancy between her outer appearance and her strong character. Her personality traits were evident in her glance, manner of speaking, and movements. Mila was a woman of low height perhaps even miniature height, and was very elegant. There was something teenage-like about her figure, and her modest clothing only highlighted this. Later, I learnt that Mila bought most of her clothes from a children's store.

She had short hair and stubborn curls. Hergrey eyes viewed each person with an unhidden, even childish, curiosity. One could notice a slight vigilance in the way she turned her head and moved her lips. Mila never let go of her pen and would always be writing something. After some time, I learnt that she paid attention to detail, and during my talks with her, I understood how important that was for her.

During our collaboration, Mila and I became close. I started to analyse events, paying attention to detail in a similar way to Mila, it allowed me to find unexpected results. Gradually, diving deep into the data of conducted studies, as if moving along a twisting labyrinth by trial and error, we managed to approach the result that to some degree, helped us explain the studied phenomenon. It was interesting and exciting. Considering the fact that it was possible to process the obtained data outside the institute, I offered to let Mila stay at my place for a while. Besides, it was the middle of winter and Mila couldn't shift her chronic cold. She lived in an uncomfortable dormitory with two young women and, from what I understood, it was far from being perfect.

Since we began to share an apartment, we became even closer. I respected Mila's devotion to her work, as well as her uncompromised exactness in making the results clear, and her hard work when it came to analyzing controversial data. Moreover, I saw more and more of Mila's personality, especially how she was in everyday life, outside of the laboratory. In a rough-and-ready fashion, we cooked meals and drank tea in the evenings. From our talks, I learnt much about this closed off and restraint girl; about her childhood in a small village, where her father was a school teacher. After Mila finished the second grade, she and her family moved to the district centre. Her parents, very humbly, lived in a tiny apartment with their two daughters, and it was a happy time for Mila. She always missed that house, where she felt warm and comfortable. Such memories never fade, and nostalgia always chooses the most vulnerable moments to remind people.

Mila's elder sister stayed at their parents' apartment with her family to support their father after their mother died. After finishing university and receiving a distinction in her degree,, Mila stayed at the university department. In several years, she produced her dissertation, and the research we were analyzing could become the basis of her doctoral thesis. When our relationship became more trustful, I learnt that, despite her age of 32, Mila's life was filled with studies, work, thesis defense; despair about her mother's illness and early passing; caring for her father, attachment to her elder sister, and her children. Before we met, there was no room for her personal life. With a certain sadness, Mila said that her life resembled a strict soldier's service. But reading between the lines, I could see that this small, unusual woman with a pure soul, just like each of us, hoped to fully experience happiness.

After some time, we finally reached the logical end of processing the obtained data. Mila suggested sending our materials to the international conference. We embodied this idea and sent our results the day before the deadline. Within a month, we were surprised to receive the message that our report had been accepted and rewarded with a grant. The organization committee provided us with tickets and a stay in one of the central hotels of Istanbul, where the conference was held. Moreover, we didn't need to pay the admission fee for this scientific forum. Of course, we took this offer as an honour, and got ourselves ready for the trip. Besides aiming to successfully deliver the report - which we were preparing thoroughly, under the control of Mila's pedantic standards - we also wanted to look good. Mila sewed herself a costume from a tight, fine silk and knitted a grey poncho - the weather forecast predicted cold snaps.

After a fussy preparation for the international forum, we found ourselves flying to Istanbul by Turkish airlines and anticipated the coming events with a sinking heart. Organizers of the conference were meeting us at the airport, and Mila, distrusting of strangers, warned me not to believe everyone who knew our surnames. On our way to the hotel, I could feel her inner tension which started to gradually disappear only when we reached our hotel room. Everything about this trip to Istanbul was exciting. We found ourselves in this new and unknown land, with its traditions and laws. We immediately decided to explore the city. We agreed with a local taxi driver that we could actively move around the city with him driving us. Our driver's name was Marat and he was a loving guy. He let me sit in the front seat, highlighting this country's respect for female figures. In his imperfect attempt at speaking Russian, he would repeat, "Money isn't important. It's important that people see whom I drive."Marat showed us the city. It was especially pleasant when, after the gala-dinner, a special cortege was accompanying honorable guests, and Marat was the first to join the escort of honor and take the Ukrainian delegates.

The trip was truly amazing, filled with meeting, and speaking to, new people; interesting reports at the conference, excursions, and the discovery of a new culture and its traditions. Everything merged into a single joyful flow of unforgettable impressions. It would have been so great to stop that moment, but the minutes had flown away like birds near Bosporus. We had part of the money left from our financial reward and by the end of our stay there, we asked Marat to take us to a nice place, where we could buy some high-quality clothes . We were driving out of Istanbul, when, after some silence, Mila announced,

"Here we go, we're on our way to our destinations: you're going to a harem and I – to a factory."

After a short pause, Marat parried:

"Don't count on it."

Finally, we reached a collection of large stores with beautiful and bright shop-windows, situated on a large barren land. In one of them, someone opened a door for us and upon entering, we saw multiple sheepskin coats, fur coats and overcoats of very good quality. A young and attractive man approached us. He was the owner of this store and his name was Antonio. He was of Italian origin and was very proud of everything that was happening in his "little kingdom."

I chose a sheepskin coat for myself and quickly became filled with the positivity of shopping. Besides, I had a keen desire to purchase something interesting for Mila. Antonio was joking with us and offered us some good Turkish coffee. I'd like to note here that before our trip, experienced people had been instructing us and advising to strongly object any attempts to give us any sort of treat. That is why, in unison, Mila and I would refuse everything. Trying to gain Antonio's favor, I started to tell him about Mila's merits as a scientist and about her excellent taste that, unfortunately, didn't always correspond with her opportunities. In my opinion, he understood everything I had said, and he asked a very precise question,

"Do you want a sheepskin coat or an overcoat?"

I replied, in a laid-back manner,

"An overcoat. Varnished, slender and elegant. One that fits her."

Antonio asked Mila to take off her poncho to determine her shape. Then he suddenly turned to me and asked,

"Will you drink some whiskey with me?"

Understanding the significance of forming a trustful relationship, I didn't have the right to refuse. Antonio commanded someone to bring a coat to Mila. She was brought a slender coat of varnished leather and she carefully put it on. Elegantly outlining her small figure, it turned this fragile woman into a touching, sweet princess with a sparkling smile. Antonio and I froze with surprise. We saw a completely new person stood before us. When we started discussing prices with Antonio, it became clear that even if we pooled the money of both of us, we wouldn't have had enough for half of this coat.

"Antonio, listen. We don't have the necessary sum. But think, you can make this woman happy. You will remember it forever. And even in the hardest days it will make you joyful, keep your soul warm, and satisfy your self-respect."

Antonio looked at me cunningly and asked,

"Will you come on a vacation with me?"

I gladly replied,

"Of course, but next year."

Antonio gave me a pack of his business cards, hoping that at least one of them would remind me of him. When the coat was packed, I felt incredible joy. After saying goodbye, Antonio chased us onto the street and gave Mila a small leather purse. It was very touching. We were returning home with new memories and hopes - anticipating happy changes. Custom officers looked at us with understanding when we came to the airport wearing a sheepskin coat and a leather coat in the middle of May.

***

As usual, spring and summer ended quickly. Mila and I met in October. She was wearing a beautiful leather coat, high heels, and carrying a small purse in her hands. I couldn't take my eyes from Mila. She had changed so much! When I saw her closer, I noticed the energy bursting out of her eyes. They were shining and I realised – Mila was in love!

Mila told me that only recently she, an opponent of accidental acquaintances, wearing her new coat, had met a man on the street and now, she couldn't imagine her life without him. When I met him, I noted that in his presence, Mila was radiating light, and he turned from a tough man into a smiley, happy guy who was constantly readjusting his expensive glasses and glancing attentively at his life's companion.

***

They have lived together for 7 years already. This year, their son will go into first grade. When I reunited with Mila at one of the conferences, she gave me a hug and said, "Life can turn into a fairytale. I'd never believe that something like that could happen to me. Can you believe it, I'm falling in love with Yura more and more after years." We recalled Antonio with warmth at heart and realized, once again, that our gratitude would be reaching him through our memories for many years to come…

Snow Outside the Window

Every time I start communicating with a new patient, it's hard to guess what meaning the conversation will bring to me. In the fuss of scheduled work days, and everyday chores, one can't always stop to perceive the meaning of events. People cross your path, teaching you to appreciate the gift we call life in its simplest and most accessible forms. This is exactly what happened when one of my young colleagues asked me to consult a patient of, as he called it, an elegant age.

The patient was a very sophisticated woman of 48 who had coal-like eyes that seemed to see right into your soul. Olga Alexandrovna began to show me different papers with her diagnoses and results of various physical examinations. She was taking them out of a heavy folder with a certain degree of virtuosity, thus confirming the seriousness of her attitude from the very beginning of our consultation. She came to me in the hopes of finding a likeminded person to solve her problems, so that she could start to feel confident again. And she had her reasons. In the past, Olga Alexandrovna had had several large and complicated surgeries - craniotomy because of a brain tumor, a removal of one of the kidneys based on an oncological disease. She had to overcome all of this during 3 years.

Undoubtedly, this experience left its trace and she had trouble when communicating - pronouncing words with visible difficulty. And her left arm and leg were limited in movements. I talked with her for a long time, touching on everyday questions and not only medical ones. During our consultation, I learnt much about her life. Her destiny resembled many others, but the burden of hardships and diseases made her story special. In the meantime, she didn't talk about it like it was a serial drama. She met a lot of good people in these memorable places.

I quickly realized that her smile, and the love in her voice, allowed her to set completely different tones on dramatic events, making them seem less harsh. Olga Alexandrovna was a teacher in primary grades of a school in the city, and she frequently mentioned how much she loved her work. My patient didn't have children of her own, and during our talks, I understood that the school was her home. She would say, "There are no difficult children. Children are always good from the very beginning. We have to remember that and give them the opportunity to open up. Difficult children become dear to me. With them, I'm trying to reach their true goodness."

Besides, Olga Alexandrovna had an incredible sense of humour. In her flowing speech, she nonchalantly emphasised the 'elements of funny actions'. She talked about them with such urgency that it seemed to me they were the most important part of her story. After examining her, I understood that my patient needed another surgery… I tried to help her make a hard decision, but whilst talking to her, I became convinced that Olga Alexandrovna wasn't surprised about this diagnosis. We chose the day of hospitalisation and discussed the details of her examination and surgery preparations. Olga Alexandrovna insisted that anesthesia would be administered by the doctor she knew well after her previous surgery in our institute. Everything was put into play considering all of her requirements, and on the scheduled day, my patient came to our department.

When I visited her on the hospital ward before the surgery, she was sitting on her bed, wrapped up into a terry robe that was too big for her. Her feet in knitted socks hung childishly down the bed, not reaching the floor. Her small slippers with huge pom poms looked funny and cocky. Her boyish hair, disheveled more than usual, and her black eyes were shining brighter than ever. We talked about the wonderful weather outside, about the forthcoming holidays, and about the fact that she'd be taken to the surgery room in about 30-40 minutes.

Everything went as usual: surgery and post-surgical period. Considering the uncommon situation, we provided Olga with an individual post-surgical ward. It was a ward with large, uncurtained windows that Olga Alexandrovna later called potholes. Outside the window, snow was falling. Near the door of my office, a grey-haired stocky man of medium height was waiting for me, anxiously flicking through a magazine he held in his hands. It was Olga Alexandrovna's husband. I tried to calm him down and explained that the biggest problems were in the past. Everything was fine, and Olga Alexandrovna would be transferred to a common ward the next day.

He looked at me very attentively. It seemed to me that he was trying not to miss out anything serious in our conversation – some doctors tend to hide things between the lines. But in this case, I could let myself be sincere. As a farewell, he said to me,

"You know, every time I'm waiting for her, I'm asking God to forgive us... I ask Him to take away her illnesses. I'd like to take them all onto me. She's like a baby. Even the children at school are her friends."

***

The next day, I came to the ward where Olgat had been transferred to from the resuscitation department. There, I saw a woman with bright, whitish hair that was tightened in a knot on her back of the head. She looked bossy, sitting on a chair near a bed, her arms crossed on her breast. She had black eyebrows and widely-set eyes, where I could see the familiar shining. It was my patient's mother. Right after we greeted each other, Olga Alexandrovna was brought into the ward. She had already become rather active and was appreciative of everything – my explanations; preparation of the IV dropper; the small flower that was standing in a glass on a bedside table - evidently brought by her mother - and the buzz of the air conditioner. She exclaimed that the noise of the air conditioner reminded her of rain When she saw it was snowing, she exclaimed, .

"This snow is so unusual. It's so beautiful! It makes me so happy to see it."

***

In the post-surgical period, every day is meaningful. IEvery individual deals with it differently. They have to allow themselves to feel the emotions and sensations left behind by their experience.

***

Olga Alexandrovna's post-operational period took a normal course without any complications. By virtue of her active life and incredible optimism, she turned all natural hardships of that time into small 'discoveries and souvenirs of life'. In optimism, she managed to take her first steps, drink a glass of water herself, and style her hair. Thanks to this amazing woman, I learnt how bright and meaningful each moment of our life could be. Underestimating the transiency of being, we steal from ourselves, and come back to appreciating the simplest things only after getting into difficult life situations.

Olga Alexandrovna embraced the changes of each new day with the joyfulness of a child, and with unhidden delight. The days of her stay in the clinic went by quickly, and again, I felt the sensation of emotional fulfilment from the peculiarity that distinguishes our job from many others. In particular, this peculiarity is the ability to help people eliminate their problems. That's the way the world works: a doctor, in a sense, becomes closer than anyone else to a patient during illness. This virtue of trustful human interaction sometimes brings the most different people together for many years, and leaves an unforgettable trace on the soul.

When Olga Alexandrovna's husband came into my office, his eyes were shining with happiness, making him look much younger than he had looked on our first meeting.

"I'm so happy that I can take my dear Olga home today. The waiting gets more difficult after each time, there's not enough endurance for everything."

Within several minutes, Olga Alexandrovna entered my office, too. Despite the fact that she had lost some weight after the surgery, she looked light and happy. She was returning home with the feeling of hope after her ordeal. I gave her recommendations for the next few months. When Olga Alexandrovna approached the door, she turned back to say,

"I didn't want to tell you before, but now I can. When I was preparing for the surgery, I made a decision: in light of the reality of the effects of oncological problems, I wanted it all to end. I even begged the anesthesiologist to help me ... And when I woke up and saw the snow outside the window... It was so perfect, just like the simplest things in this life... And now, I don't want to shorten or miss out on any time I have left."

She opened the door, behind which her husband was waiting for her and the two of them hurried home.

***

Through the window I observed how carefully he was helping her sit into their car. The left the clinic and the snow kept on falling outside the window. I recalled that New Year's Eve was coming. And it meant that I could have my own new beginning.

Smile of a Newfoundland Dog

That morning, Regina woke up earlier than usual. For several days, her soul had been disturbed like a flame in the wind. The easy life she had worked hard to achieve was gone in an instant. Through thoughts, she continued to return to the moment she first met the glance of the man. The man, who managed to read her soul entirely in an instant, understand her and raise her spirits. This meeting launched the chain reaction of interrelated and unpredictable events that changed all of the past and her, seemingly, unshakable views on life.

She hurried to plunge herself into a new day. And joyfulness took over everything she was feeling, because in this world - such a cruel, cold and yet seemingly predictable world - everything changes and becomes brighter once you catch a glimpse of magic at work. Regina got up from her bed and recalled how her granny used to wake her up early in the morning when she was a little girl and take her to their front garden to walk barefoot on the ground. . She placed her feet onto her carpet, wanting to relive the experience. She recalled the forgotten world of childhood sensations and discoveries. It happened so long ago, as if in another world or another life.

Impregnated with rain, fog was spreading in water-based paints outside the window. Purple-pink asters in a transparent vase and their pointed petals awoke her memories of her parents' home. Regina looked at her watch, and for the first time in many years, noticed with surprise that the minute and second hands on her clock dial had an unusual glow – habitual things started to look different. Music was playing in her soul. These changes never ceased to surprise her. When she went to visit her friend, and met her son - whom she had heard so much about, and whom she could envisage due to the pictures she had seen - everything changed. And their 30-minute talk, like a flow of vital energy, opened the door to yet another unseen world. And she entered this door.

***

Regina recently turned 29, and she had worked for an embassy for a couple of years. Despite the certain fixedness of her work, and its requirement for strict adherence to subordination, Regina liked her everyday activities. She had to talk to different and, as a rule, interesting people and it filled every day with meaning. But giving herself entirely to her work, she started to, more frequently, feel the growing emptiness in her home that she had been trying to fill with warmth and comfort. When communicating, Regina preferred laconism and accuracy leaving out any possibility to penetrate into her inner world. Grey and black colors dominated her wardrobe. Even when she was dressing herself and doing her makeup, her actions were accurate and consecutive. All algorithms were well-tested and her self-control in everything became the basis of her life.

Regina approached the mirror and, looking at herself attentively, saw a young woman she didn't know. Big eyes of violet colour, framed by long eyelashes, were looking at her. Her well-groomed eyebrows highlighted her good taste. Her straight nose, with a small bump made her profile special. Her freckles, which were attractively scattered across her white skin, sometimes dissolved in her flushed cheeks. Her distinctly outlined lips had two small folds on the sides, but it didn't spoil her appearance. Curls of red hair fell on her shoulders. Her high forehead was hidden by her fringe. Maybe she should let it grow? Dimples appeared on her cheeks, and when the young woman smiled, her face began to glow.

It was a weekend, and Regina was going to visit morning mass in a cathedral. The realisation of potential changes in her life required spiritual support. Looking at her wardrobe, she realized that the colors she used to like didn't match well with her current mood. She wanted to wear something green, something that reminded her of spring grass after rain. She carefully took her granny's emerald earrings out of a small jewel-case and put them onto her ears. A green silk scarf that she found in the depths of her wardrobe twisted around her neck several times. Seeing this change of appearance in the mirror, her eyes were sparkling with happiness and all she could feel was pleasure.

***

It is so blissful to live and know that in this world, there is a person, for whom, you want to become better for. You become vulnerable. The emerging world of emotional experiences and hopes, is connected to the real world by a thin thread, thinner than spidery lace. A tsunami of feelings can connect these worlds, but what if the thread breaks and that notorious world of feelings and hopes remains virtual? The desire to turn these dreams into reality, surpasses all the resources of this world. After a taste of the happiness you can attain, it's so hard to return to the grey, everyday life.

***

It is so amazing to travel through one's own thoughts, moving at any distance and into any time. Regina felt a nagging sadness out of uncertainty and waiting. She hadn't received any messages from Oleg in three weeks. What happened to him? Where was he? What did this silence mean? This man, with whom she talked with for only half an hour, entered her life and now his absence could be felt in everything. But he promised he would find her.

She was hurrying to the Cathedral of St. Alexander like a thirsty traveller wanting to quench his thirst. Stepping into the cathedral her soul eased. She felt better. After mass, she went outside into the autumn day; patches of sunlight on the multicolored, leaves, a cloudless blue sky. A woman was moving towards her, with a big dog by her side. Regina came abreast with the Newfoundland and looked back to see it again. And suddenly the dog also turned to her and… smiled!

It was a good sign. It was a miracle. With each cell of her body, Regina felt that everything would be fine in her life from then onwards…

***

"Hello! Hi, it's me!"
"Where have you been for so long?!"

And happiness burst into their life with the first whirlwinds of the coming winter.

Eternity

Rays of a lazy autumn sun were breaking through the large windows of the lecture hall. The light filled every crack of the room, which still felt unfamiliar to Nina. It had been a week since she began her studies at the Kharkov Medical University.. A bit more than a month before, she and her mother had visited this big city with sliding trams. The familiar railway station of Zhmerynka, where her grandmother lived, greeted them. They jumped into the train carriage whilst running not to miss it (it stopped only for 5 minutes) and dragged an unwieldy suitcase that they previously used only when going to the sea. Nina was prudent and had filled it with books on physics, chemistry and biology. And, despite being able to pass only one exam and still succeed, she hardly believed she had gotten into a respectable university on her first application. But it happened.

Nina's mother smiled knowingly, observing her daughter, who was at the height of concentration, the daughter who had protected herself from the world's hardships with her piles of books. Nina still believed that they could guide her into happiness. And she considered having the chance to move to this city, live among these people, and have countless opportunities, the greatest thing. It was almost like breaking through the looking-glass.

During her childhood and adolescent years, she was filled with the joy of a small-town paradise, and she absorbed the love of its dear people and their sincerity. The life of each family was unfolding in front of everyone; people were like an open book. The mutual perception of any meaningful event was reigning there. Joy, surprise, accusation and hostility – everything was common. That is why, if something unusual happened in this small hive, it became alive and saturated with the unity of common emotions and actions.

Nina plunged into the memories of cold and crispy winters with mysterious frosty figures on the windows. She recollected purple-crimson evenings, strings of frozen linen blowing with the freshness of a chilly wind, the warmth coming from the logs that were burning in a stove. She always considered herself the happiest person because she was an indispensable part of this town..

Nina rejoiced every time spring visited her hometown. She and her little sister, Zhenya, would put on their rubber boots, and walk till late at night near a river that was flowing not far from their house. From the beginning of summer, everything became bright with colour. And in the mornings, waking up with the sunrise, she wanted to run to the garden to stand barefooted on the morning dew. Enjoying the scattering rays of the rising sun breaking through the morning fog.

She would look back on these childhood memories for her entire life.

***

She was now standing in a noisy lecture hall filled with students, whom she had already met from the first weeks of studies. For a week, after studying, she had been going to a hotel, where she stayed with her mother during exams. This room was one of the only places she felt at home in this new city. Nina sat in the second to last row of the lecture room, observing everyone else fill in the remaining rows. In the center of the room, there was a group of girls who apparently knew each other very well. They held themselves with pride, and, as Nina thought, wore queen's dresses. A red-headed guy, who was sitting nearby, noticed Nina's concentrated gaze and whispered,

"Local beauties."

The girls were watching their classmates who were walking nearby, as if reassuring themselves they were still centre of attention. Nina casted a glance onto her new boots that her mom had bought from a local market. She realised that shoes were more comfortable than beautiful: a thick, sturdy sole, and long dark shoelaces tied into a large bow. Nina felt the urge to hide her feet under the table.

An old dressmaker, her grandmother's friend, Aunt Dosya, had sown a blouse for Nina, but to her own taste, and in accordance with the fashion at that time. It was made out of striped fabric and had a tongue-like collar. It looked funny, somehow lonely and awkward. A tube-like sundress was chosen to tone the strips on her blouse. The outfits she wore always made her look older.

Nina examined the students who were entering into the lecture hall, and her fear of the changes in store was replaced with a desire to actively participate. Only a few minutes were left before the beginning of the lecture. A young man, who resembled a divine being to Nina, entered the hall. He was tall and smiley and had a mop of unruly, dark hair that fell on his shoulders. He was listening attentively to a student who had approached him. Even though his robe was a bit rumpled, it looked tight on his broad shoulders and highlighted his athletic figure. His eyebrows, merged on his bridge of nose, were rising during the conversation which was interrupted by his loud and booming laughter every now and then. This young man intrigued Nina..

Nina felt as if a ball of lightning had struck her, affecting her state, her thoughts, her life, past and present; confusing everything. She suddenly felt incredibly anxious. Nina was scared to even look at this amazing young man, whose name she had learnt was Jules. This name seemed to be as magical and amazing as its holder.

The red-headed young man from earlier, introduced himself as Konstantin, and once again, brought Nina out of her thoughts. He explained that Jules was a student from Israel. In their group, there were more foreign students than anywhere else, most of them coming from Arabic countries.

To Nina, they were people from another world, or even from other planets. She was both excited and fearful when she imagined communicating with them.

The next day, whilst she was meeting her classmates, she spotted Jules and two other foreign students at a small table (the two other students being Husam from Jordan, and Nasim from Israel). Konstantin, pointed at an empty chair nearby with the simplicity and likeability of an old friend. Ninatook a seat, trying to hide herself behind her large briefcase.

Nina noticed how three girls in mini-robes looked at her with unhidden smiles. Without any words, she could understand their desire to discuss Nina's appearance and unconfident behaviour. Nearby, three students were talking loudly. All of them were from Kharkov and it was evident that they weren't really interested in what was happening in the lecture hall. Jules was the first to break the silence. He gazed at Nina, not hiding his surprise.

"What's your name?"
"I'm Nina,"
"I'm Jules. Why are you shaking?"
"I'm afraid, but I don't know why,"
"How old are you?"
"Sixteen."

Everyone looked at Nina. Her bag slipped from her knees, fell onto the floor and her notebooks fell out of it. Nina started picking them up and Jules was helping her. Jules looked at her with interest and burst out into loud laughter. To her own amazement, she asked him,

"Can I call you Julien? It's a name I know from foreign literature."

Jules laughed even harder, "Of course, my dear."

Nina felt dizzy at his use of "dear". It felt like the entire world had froze. She looked at Jules and realised she had found herself in a black hole that was impossible to get out of. This was the start of her journey at Kharkov Medical University. She settled into the dormitory where she shared a room with two more girls. One of them was from Lebanon and another one – from Belgorod. Despite the numerous difficulties she faced adapting into her new life, it was also a happy time, because Jules lived on the same floor. It meant that Nina could talk to him not only in the university, but after classes, also.

She feared the feelings she found herself experiencing, as well as the unpredictable actions that she sometimes couldn't control. Nina opened herself up to a new world of relationships; she really wanted to change her appearance, and become an interesting person to talk to. She didn't have any problems with her studies, and she immediately became a leader in her group. She liked to study and absorb new knowledge. Everything related to it was habitual and understandable. What she needed to fix was the contrast of her appearance compared to her classmates'.

At first, one of her classmates, Marina, advised Nina to remove her eyebrows and - using an eyebrow pencil draw thin threads, to make them resemble those of the women from the times of Leonardo da Vinci. Gullibly, and even with some enthusiasm, Nina decided to take on board this advice, and the next day, became the cause of laughter for all her classmates. Only Jules was looking at Nina attentively and, seeing that she was ready to burst into tears, instructed her to sit beside him, reprimanding her for her gullibility. Then, he took her by the hand, led her out of the lecture hall, and wiped away the drawn eyebrows using his handkerchief. Her face was wet because of tears. She felt hurt, ashamed and bitter. Looking into the eyes of Jules' she felt the infinity of their journey was nothing compared to reality.

Jules smiled and, putting his forefinger in front of his face, said quietly,

"Don't do it!"

She strove to hide her feelings, but the eloquence of her gaze and the glow she exhibited in front of Jules couldn't be unnoticed by others… It seemed to Nina that the only person who didn't notice her feelings was the most important one – Jules, himself. He treated her with respect and unhidden interest. He liked to share banter with her and write her funny notes. Nina kept them all in a secret box and reread them before falling asleep.

Her first study year ended.

Nina returned home to her romantic paradise, taking along an electric stove she brought for her family on the money she saved. She had only excellent marks in her record book, joy from returning home in her soul, and endless love in her heart.

***

Nina was observing her hometown, after returning from another dimension, and the sensation of inner changes could be felt with each step. Walking along the streets, where she knew every single house and every single stone lying on the ground, she felt nagging anguish. She ran through the gate of her home . Everything was familiar here, but it didn't seem as big as it was in her childhood. Her mom, sister and Granny were standing on the threshold waiting. The whirlwind of inner delight, joy and happiness made these moments unforgettable.

In the hospitable, warm home, amongst her near and dear people, time flew incredibly fast. Once again, Nina realized that our mood, state of the soul, as well as the absence of a real opportunity to slow down events, had a significant influence on this universal notion that we call time.

***

When Nina entered the lecture hall after summer holidays, many people didn't recognize her. She had changed. Her childish plumpness and insecure movements of an ugly duckling had disappeared. She had become thinner and even seemed to be taller. Her hair, carefully styled into a pageboy cut that was very popular at the time, highlighted the beautiful oval of her face, and her long neck resembled Modigliani's women. Her dark-complexion seemed to keep her inner light contained. It gushed through her wide, grey eyes.

Nina was wearing a black dress with white dots. It emphasized her shape - which had changed for the better - and had smooth folds that were falling below her knees. A thread of artificial white pearls bore a resemblance to her white shiny teeth that would close into a joyful smile, revealing dimples on her cheeks. Her manner of speaking, and the way she looked at the people she conversed with, had also changed. She gave the impression that her restraint manner in relationships with others was required to protect the intrinsic trust she held for everyone. There was only one thing that hadn't changed. Her eyes still sparkled when she saw Jules.

He also started treating her differently, altering his cocky manner of talking, to a scrutinizing, reserved sympathy. Nina could look at him forever, examining each freckle on the thin skin of his face. She was happy to gaze at him during class, where he could easily analyse any situation.

He told Nina about his mother, his big family and the hometown he missed so much. Once, Jules said that before death, a person could see main events from his life like in a film. Nina found herself thinking that their first kiss would more than likely feature in this film.

She fell ill. It was cold in the dorm and, going out to the kitchen to get a teapot in a winter evening, she was sure that she wouldn't see Jules because he had left for Moscow. Her throat was covered with a scarf, she wore Granny's knitted socks, and was wrapped inside a shawl. She looked at the snow falling outside the window, dissolving in the evening twilight. Someone hugged her and she suddenly felt dizzy. Jules, stricken by her look, stood behind her.

"You remind me of the funniest child in the world. My favorite child. I'd like to take this illness away from you…"

He hugged Nina and clasped her in his arms. Their first kiss possessed the eternity of unforgettable and inimitable happiness - when it's possible to easily lose one's ground and hover in the infiniteness of space, with total disregard of gravity laws. She felt her soul fly. All of her years in the university were filled with this immense happiness that surpassed all limits. However, the 6 years passed quickly.

***

Jules had to continue his education in a graduate school and Nina had to go to outlying districts to start work as a doctor. He explained to her that for the time being, he couldn't be the master of his own destiny because he had to put the people who had sent him to study in front of himself. In the meantime, Nina's granny died and her mother fell seriously ill, so she had to move closer to her parents' house. For some time, she felt that her world had been destroyed. Warm, sunny colors left, and everything acquired greyish shades. Even the people around her seemed to talk using other tones. She was working for days, living most of her life in the hospital. Sometimes, it seemed to her that she was in a war, with battles that secretly unfolded in the dull everyday life.

Once, being amongst endless calls, patients and suffering people, Nina felt unbearable anguish over Jules. Leaving everything behind, she left for the closest district center to get a train ticket to Kharkov. She got onto the train gave way to the tears she couldn't hold anymore. The train felt incredibly slow, with too many pointless stops.

Getting to Kharkov's railway station, she took a taxi and hurried to the dorm along the familiar streets. Nina flew past a front-door security man and pulled on the door she knew so well. She was knocking, crying, and then she just squatted down nearby, realising in a single moment that everything that had previously existed in her life had turned into a mirage. The security man, who remembered her very well, gave Nina some tea and told her that the day before, Jules had left for Minsk to continue his education there.

Happy people, and especially lovers, are always careless. They plunge into the depths of their feelings, not noticing the events happening around. When Nina parted with Jules, she didn't learn the address of his family and, out of her carelessness, didn't give her's to him. The letters she sent to the dorm didn't reach the destination for a strange reason. Everything favoured the fact that they couldn't meet at that point in their lifetime. Nina returned to her small town life with a desire to change something in it. She dissolved in the people who were close to her and who supported her, feeling their sincerity and sympathy.

Having worked for several years, Nina left for Kiev to a capital clinic for further education. There she met her future husband and gained a foothold in her job. When she fell pregnant, she felt that her life had acquired meaning. When she was in the 7_{th} month, she fell ill with a severe infectious disease and, being in almost unconscious state in the resuscitation department, she dreamt only of her child. In the first days after her recovery, her husband brought her a strange letter that, by some miracle, had arrived at Nina's home address. For a long time, she didn't dare to open it, seeing the familiar handwriting on the envelope. And, reading the first lines, she couldn't hold back her tears.

Jules was looking for her and, having found her contact details, wrote her right away. He wrote that he missed her, that everything around him seemed insipid, that work didn't save him and that he had recently defended his thesis. He also wrote that he had had a dream, where Nina was lying in a white robe and couldn't speak or move. He wanted to see her and, considering a certain degree of difficulty of his movements as a foreign citizen, he asked her to come to Minsk.

Nina had a premature birth and the girl who was born at sunrise, required her total care. She took her baby and left for her home town. In their deserted house, she lived with her mother who had been seriously sick for some time. It seemed that days and nights merged into one, when tiny Masha couldn't fall asleep and a lamp was burning near her mother's bed.

Once, on a Christmas night, Nina wrote a letter to Jules, where she gave way to her pain and her worries. She rewrote it several times, throwing the sheets of paper into the burning stove one by one. Many lines were becoming blurred because her tears were falling on the paper. In the morning, Nina sealed the envelope and took it to the post office. She did it quickly, fearing that someone could prevent her from doing it. A week later she received a letter, where he shared his endless happiness that they could at least write to each other. He was asking her to take care of herself and of Masha. Instead of a farewell, he wrote that her letter for him was like a fire on a cold and damp night. He was waiting for her.

A few days later, her mother died. After the funeral, Nina came back to the big city with Masha and started her life anew.

***

15 years passed.

Nina's family life wasn't successful. She divorced her husband when Masha went into first grade. Nina defended her Candidate's dissertation and became the head of one of the therapeutic clinics. She deserved to gain authority among her colleagues and patients, being certain in the simple truth that one's devotion to responsibilities and benevolence toward people would never let her fail. She gave all her unspent love to Masha. The rhythm of her everyday life, with strict chronology and predictability became routine.

She returned back home after a hard day at work and was listening to Masha's speeches. Masha was a creative girl who liked art and poetry. She inherited her mother's benevolence and openness, having her own opinion on everything. They lived in the world they created by themselves. It was filled with warmth and trustful sincerity. Love, transferred to Nina from her mother and grandmother, reigned in their house. And, despite the presence of everyday problems, everything was subjected to one main thing – mutual understanding and maintenance of their home's comfort. The phone rang. Masha called Nina to it with a surprise.

"It's some man. Speaks with an accent."

Nina froze, hearing the unforgettable sound of his voice.

"Hi! How are you? How is Masha?"

It was Jules. He came like an alien from space.

Nina talked to him for a long time, and it seemed that the entire world was coming alive, and dried gardens were returning to life. He learnt her phone number from one of his patients, an emigrant from Ukraine, who had been her patient for a long time before that. The opportunity of having this communication, even without a hint of any changes, was a priceless gift by itself.

After defending his dissertation, Jules came back to his hometown, was married, strove for several years to legalise his certificate of degree and, over time, managed to succeed in his profession. He had two sons and it seemed that his life was successful. "Everything is fine, but I don't feel the unique meaning of time. I've lost it… I'm sorry."

***

10 more years passed.

The world changed and relationships between people also changed. There was the impression that everyone had jumped onto a high-speed train that was running with no stops. It was impossible to go out of it. On that day, Nina woke up earlier than usual and recalled that she had seen Jules in her dream. He came to her, exhausted and worn out, asking her to wash away the dust from him…

She dialed Jules' number and was greeted with a sad voice.

"I'm just tired. You've been calling me only by my name recently. But you should call me Julien , as you used to."

After the morning ward round, Nina called him again. No one answered.

Jules answered after a week. He had had a heart attack. A month later, Nina flew to Israel. She took a travel tour to see his hometown, walk along his home streets and breathe his air…

And to meet him…

***

She was standing at the foot of the Bahai gardens and he was waiting for her on the top. He was coming down to her, layer by layer, and talking on the phone, she was asking him not to worry. They met after so many years in one of the most beautiful corners of the Earth, and felt that everything in the world had its meaning: everything they had experienced in their lives and everything that was yet to come. They resembled two travelers who had just overcome a desert.

After their embraces, overpowering the difficulty of the reunion after years of separation, he took out a beautiful package and gave it to her.

"You had a birthday yesterday. It's your perfume. You'll see. Eternity."

Nina, smelling the perfume, gazed at him with endless questions, not being able to focus, and recall the meaning of this word.

"It is eternity."
It was their eternity…

Smell of the Long-Gone Spring

It was a long winter. During the day, the snow was thawing in streams and drippings. As the sun began to set, water was becoming frozen in the greyish twilight. Cold hoarfrost was stubbornly appearing in windows and surfaces of puddles in the streets. In the evening sky, one could still observe the disappearing thawing disc that was setting behind the horizon. Despite the time of year, it was still possible to catch the smell of early spring with the shades of awakened ground, first greens, and freshness of water.

The streets of a morning provincial town were awakening like a single mechanism. The dwellers were filling the streets and hurrying to carry out their responsibilities early in the daybreak. Small shops and workrooms were being opened; the schools and a medical college were being heated; administrative buildings were getting ready to accept a scarce number of citizens; several factories, plants, and alimentary complexes were beginning to function. Our town was multinational; respecting different traditions, manners of speaking, cooking, dressing.

Dad was the first to wake up and warm the house up - kindling the stove using the odorous logs he had prepared the day before. It was still dark outside, when specks of burning logs started playing on the walls. Everyone was gradually getting up from warm beds with starched sheets. In the yard, we heard the devoted barking of our dog,

Sharik – a dog of an unknown breed that latched onto our house several years ago.

Aunt Dasha, who was living with us, and my Mom, were cooking breakfast, arranging the table and hurrying my sister and me, who were lazily and slowly preparing for school. Half an hour later, we were running to our school, racing one another and calling our peers who lived nearby. Within 10 minutes we reached "the universal center" – this is how my first teacher Claudia Iosifovna referred to our school. I remember how we carried inkpots to class in rag handmade bags, set them down in the middle of slanted school desks with ascending folds, and used dip pens for writing. That seems so exotic today. We always had indelible ink stains on our hands that sometimes also moved to our faces.

After the bell, the curtain between classes started coming up. Today, these classes resemble the memories that floated away into the irretrievable past. It even seems that the sky was bluer, the sun was brighter, grass was greener, winters – more snowy and frosty, and the faces of our dear people – younger and happier.

I was 10 and my sister was 7, when our father, one of the surgeons working in the district hospital, decided to take us to his evening ward round. It was necessary for him to return to the hospital in the second part of the day to visit his patients once again. He loved people, he liked to be needed and helpful (he would say that without any affectedness). Since it was possible to reach the hospital by foot in 30-40 minutes, depending on the pace speed - and phones were a rare thing back then - home and work turned into a system of linked vessels. Dad could be called to the hospital at any moment and we could recognise the car with a red cross by sound, when it was driving to our house in a case of urgency. Sometimes, after a night surgery, Dad would come back home at daybreak, saturated with that smell of the hospital. He would prepare a strong black tea on a heated stove. I remember the way he would brew and drink it, how he interlaced the sips with smoking a cigarette, enjoying every moment and plunging into his own state. It all was so special and unique to me.

In these moments, despite his tiredness, he had a special magnetism. His smooth face traits, his shining, deep blue eyes, his plump lips pressed together on his swarthy face. It seemed to me that even in winter, his face was covered with slight tan. His soft, dark-blonde hair, always neatly trimmed, became grey very early. He had a medium height, was stocky and a bit plump. He always wore fine, embroidered shirts, and preferred light-coloured clothes in summer and different shades of grey for colder seasons. Hats suited him a lot, highlighting his manliness and elegance. Our father impressed people in a unique way. Every word of his had its profound meaning and there was no fuss in his presence. He could listen and sincerely empathise with whomever he was speaking to. It wasn't accidental that, when a famous actress - my favorite, Malvina Schwindler - met him, she exclaimed with unique candor that was so inherent of her, "Oksana, if I didn't know your Mom, I would very much love to whisk your dad away."

It's very likely that many other women dreamt of the same thing and it sometimes caused troubles for my Mom. But she was able to ignore it, and always remained the single centre of his attention. Being a thoughtful companion, he was also a brilliant lecturer. He read a lot and had been collecting books for all his life. After his death, we donated the most part of our library to the Gaysin's medical college, according to his wish. My father, Verpakhovsky Vasiliy Franzevich, was a war child; a boy who experienced early life in a guerrilla band and all the troubles of that time. After finishing school, he entered the Vinnitsa Medical University, became a Komsomol leader and, with his readiness for hardships, decided to improve the county medicine. He left for Gaysin, together with my Mom, Alla Nikolayevna – a beautiful woman who was known not only for her bright appearance and soft personality, but also for her amazing soprano.

In Gaysin, they started their work in an old hospital built by a local landowner before the Revolution. It was the town where they spent the biggest part of their happy, and often dramatic, life. We lived very modestly, but the love we experienced from all our family members was incredible. It was a time of happiness, filled with warmth of dear people, endless holidays and bright, everyday life. We were friends with all the children who lived in the district. We invented so many games and created numerous far-fetched fantasies. It was an unforgettable discovery of the world, ourselves and our dear people living in it. Undoubtedly, it was the time of heroes. We invented names of heroes ourselves and wanted to resemble them.

Our parents gave us complete freedom. Due to their incredible busyness (our Mom was a pediatrician and also spent much time at work), we communicated much with our Aunt Dasha. To be precise, her name was Daria Avdeyevna Zadachina. She came into our family by will of an unusual event and remained with us until her old age. When my little sister Valya was born and our Mom had to return to work, she had to find a babysitter. And it was hard to find someone whom they could trust with two little children at that time. Besides, Mom strongly objected the tradition of bringing children up in specialised child care institutions. She often repeated, "Don't take away childhood from the kids."

Our grandmother, our Mom's mother, Petryk Yevgenia Ivanovna, always thought that her daughter deserved a better life and a better husband. She rarely came to visit us (she lived with our grandfather in Zhmerinka). She and our Dad had some discrepancy of opinions. She had a habit of demonstratively expressing her indignation when we couldn't recognise the fragments of her favorite music pieces and poems. She liked to eat lunch in a restaurant, wear beautiful clothes and had different chiffon kerchiefs wrapped over her head like a turban. She always pinned an elegant brooch to her collar, thus highlighting the sophistication of her every outfit.

In the evening, she freed her thick, wavy, hair, letting it fall onto her round shoulders. At these moments, we saw another Granny – a soft, joyous, and charming teller of incredible stories and fairytales. She often repeated to our parents, "Teach arts to your children, let them understand the beauty, or they will grow up into grey morally deprived persons." Traditionally, she would finish this phrase with demonstrative indignation, "It's hard to create a personality. And it's easy to break it!"

Granny's values didn't always coincide with our visions of beauty and traditions of the street that became our native environment. This was where we learnt to wash our feet in a washstand, drink water from the purling tap in the morning; eat half-raw potatoes baked in the front garden on sticks with onions; nibble on icicles, and broaden our consciousness with untraditional vocabulary. When a piano appeared in our house, our granny would indignantly say that we "mutilate its keys" with our rusty hands.

Coming back to the time when my little sister, Valya, was born, by virtue of a hopeless situation, Granny took a young woman into our house. She wasn't very tall, had small feet and hands, laughing black eyes and an Archangel manner of speaking that was unusual for us. She always wore a kerchief and a pinafore. The young woman was our beloved Aunt Dasha. After multiple visits to our friends and family members, making sure that there were no people willing to look after two children, our granny accidentally met her near a police station amongst petty hooligans. She was singing humorous rhymes, sweeping the street. She amazed our granny. She talked to her, learnt her story of her detachment from her family, and persuaded the chief police officer to let her go on her own responsibility and under the patronage of our Dad – the man well-respected by everyone in our town.

When Daria Avdeyevna came to our home, we all immediately accepted her as a family member. Mom would say that due to Aunt Dasha's compassion, diligence and innate tactfulness, she gained everyone's trust right away. Aunt Dasha was an illiterate woman. She could neither read, nor write. Our attempts to teach her weren't successful. At the same time, she knew multiple humorous rhymes and sang them proudly, theatrically rolling her eyes. She knew a lot of sayings. She cooked very tasty dishes by her own recipes. She could attentively and quietly, listen to anybody. No one knew what she was thinking at these moments. She could identify insincere and unkind people within minutes, and managed to find an opportunity to tell Dad about it in proper time. As a rule, she never was wrong. The nicknames she came up with would stick to people forever. She liked to watch TV and listen to gramophone records very much. She was never angry, but childishly surprised. And she was incredibly devoted to our family throughout her life.

Aunt Dasha would often say: "Alla Nikolayevna, the kiddies scamper around like crazy. Let's bring 'em some eats to make 'em bonnier." She called our Dad, Vasiliy Fyodorovich and respected him a lot. The name Franz was unintelligible and impossible to pronounce for her. With affected authority, after drinking at lunch, she liked to begin conversations on household topics and we were always inspired by her capacity to discuss these issues. When she saw restless movements of children fighting outside, she would go out with a stirrer for boiling the linen in her hand, and start letting out all her broad knowledge of obscene words. The street would freeze and people would stop in perplexity, hearing her pronounce these words in unbelievable combinations. And my sister and me, with a winner's expression on our red faces, would return to our yard, teasing and making faces.

We all loved her very much and couldn't imagine our house complete if she wasn't around. She helped our parents prepare us for school for the first time and then – for the graduate party. She didn't sleep at nights when we were entering universities, she married us off and even nursed my son. On the day when our father decided to take us with him for a ward round, she gave us an instructive lesson about restraint and obedience. "Go to the place where sick people lie. Don't show them that you're so witty. Everyone knows that. Listen to Vasiliy Fyodorovich – he's the main guy there." She asked us to give the pies she baked to a 7-year-old girl who had recently had a surgery.

The old building of a two-floor county hospital was located on one of the central streets of our town. A neat lane led to the heavy wooden door with figured carving. Dad came to the entrance and let us inside in front of him. And then, again, I smelt that amazing smell that often appeared in our house after our parents came back from work. I remember it well, when Dad brought us to the doctors' lounge and then we went to visit the wards together, seeing men and women after surgeries. In one of the female wards we saw a girl after an appendectomy, whom we gave Aunt Dasha's pie. She became the favourite girl of the entire department and the centre of everyone's attention. The girl was waiting for her parents to take her home, but for a strange reason, no one came. It was a severe violation of common rules.

We had the impression that we had come to a fairytale world, where illness and all other evil was driven away by the skills and knowledge of people in white robes. We felt our well-grounded inclusion in this world, and the importance of everything that took place there. White robes that fitted us well seemed to be miraculous, and our Dad – to be a wonder-worker.

Next to the hospital, there was a local cinema located on the central square. It was another amazing place in the town of my childhood. When I saw my first film there, I suppose my impressions were similar to the perception of an approaching train depicted on the screen by the Lumière brothers. We often went to the cinema and sometimes, we went to see one and the same film many times. It resembled coming to get the elixir of life. It was happiness. We knew all of the workers in the cinema and didn't doubt that they were familiar with the amazing mysteries of that place. An irreplaceable cashier, Rita Lvovna - who lived near a mill in a small private house - would always go to the cinema at its opening hours, walking through the entire town with a proudly lifted head. She highlighted her lips with a bright lipstick, which gave even more significance to her appearance. Her seriousness would gain its peak when she was gravely giving out blue tickets for the fantastic world of cinema through an opened window of her cashier desk. Those were the tickets of happiness.

One evening, Dad took us to the cinema after the ward round. They showed a movie about doctors. It was "The Degree of Risk" directed by Ilya Averbakh – the director that later became one of my favourites. Dad's colleagues were there. They greeted each other and were speaking merrily and loudly. Dad bought soda with syrup and candies for my sister and me - it was a tradition. A tall man wearing an old leather pilot jacket came into the cinema hall and put a small suitcase with worn edges and shiny fasteners on a windowsill. When he opened the suitcase lid, we saw that it was filled with small bouquets of wet violets of amazing colour and smell. These flowers were rare in our area and it was the first time my sister and I had seen them. Dad took three bouquets for my sister, myself and, as we immediately understood, for our Mom.

She came into the cinema with a flush on her face. Her wavy, thick, dark-blond hair showed from under her cap. Her beige coat was half fastened. The dimples on her cheeks accompanied her happy smile. Granny always said that Mom's lips resembled rose petals. And she was right. In that moment her shining eyes of violet color were the most amazing thing. Dad didn't take his eyes of her. Mom hugged us and when Dad gave her the bouquet of violets, she looked at him with her special gaze. It was the happiness that you learn once and can never confuse with anything else. The happiness you will always seek, overcoming grey, everyday life, wasted hopes and false expectations.

After the movie, when we came back home, we drank tea together. We told all details of the plot to Aunt Dasha, driven by her focused and serious attention. Afterwards, she put us to bed, placing the fantastic bouquets near our beds. Mom and Dad were talking about something for a long time, laughing quietly, and the atmosphere of our house was filled with a magic purple haze. In the morning, in the cool air of awakened space, we could still sense the smell of wet violets. It was the smell of happiness.

A new day was beginning. The whole world was awaiting us…

The Rose of September

Time passes by, but my memory still holds my bygone years. My darling and beloved people, who left for another world keep on living in my mind. They are a crucial part and I am their continuation. Closing my eyes and coming back into the past, again and again, I see them in front of me. I hear their voices in the transparent light of bygone events. Right now, I can see the yard of my parents' house that has already become some sort of Mecca for my soul, a path of dreams and memories on the edge of two worlds.

It was the beginning of a warm autumn. A day, satiated with ripe colors and scents coming from everything that surrounded me, creating a nostalgic warmth Sun beams were glistening on the walls, interlacing with soft lights, and filling all rooms of the house. With eye-like windows, the house was always complete with this temporary warmth, filled with the scents of autumn asters and ripe, juicy apples that were laid out on the table in a traditional bowl, and covered with unripe bunches of grapes. Mom would always put fruits on the table next to Grandma's vase with different flowers in various compositions. We could smell the fragrance of these flowers especially strongly after cleaning, when evening sun beams were dancing on white walls, and jumping to the wooden floor.

This house was cozy and light, filled with love, trust, understanding, and full of voices of people special to me. In spite of all the changes of life, it remained the keeper of peace and family warmth. The transition from the summer to the autumn is always fleeting, like the time passage in sandglass when one turns it from a horizontal to vertical position. And only clear warm evenings, with translucent nets of spider web, aweary cornflags and asters striving to prolong their triumphal time, were reminders of the forthcoming changes. Usually, during this time, my Mom and our nanny, Daria Avdeyevna, were hanging out tied corn wisps taken away from the garden, heavy wicker tails of onions, large wisps of dried fennel, and bunches of garlic, on a tense clothes-line.

We were setting out huge basins and water tanks in front of the house, where we soaked cucumbers, tomatoes and bell peppers prior to conserving them. Cabbage heads and marrows were put on buckram, next to a basket full of carrots of intense colour. Back then, my sister and I were using a special hose our Dad improvised for convenience, in order to water a small flower bed near our house. Every centimeter of this soil was filled with a great multitude of various flowers, kindly treated by my Mom's hands, who never allowed anyone, even the wise Aunt Dasha, who was involved in everything else, to handle them.

It was a real feast of multiple colours: pale-pink and crimson daisies; white, purple, and violet gillyflowers; sweet-scented tobacco with surprised heads on stalks raised above the soil; snap dragons of coralline and yellow colors (the name itself can tell us many things); standalone bushes of violet phlox; flamey torches of sages; multi-coloured grand zinnias (these flowers always reminded me of military ranks and shoulder straps); petunias that resembled little gramophones; light-blue delphiniums looking down on everything else; multicolour cornflags; lush dahlias with large heads of red and yellow colours; asters of the most different shades. Marigolds, on their thick stalks with impressive yellow flowers, were protruding in the lower layers of this captivating scenery. Being planted on the edges of flowerbeds, gillyflowers were waking up like moving, sophisticated little stars, manifesting their beauty and an amazing, fragrance that was drawing me to a mysterious land. In the twilight, the scent of the flowers would unfold itself even more, and the flower bed would acquire a new dominating shade, reaching the highest peak in the period of the dipping sunset.

Fruits and vegetables were set out in different basins with water, heated after the warm day. The more time flies, the more unreal the things happening in that space - so complex and happy at the same time - seem to be.

Rose bushes were planted in the most visible places on the flowerbed. My Mom especially loved the "Gloria day" kind, which, to her opinion, had the colour of happiness. She would always try to highlight these amazing flowers in special ways. Aunt Dasha, would call them something completely different, trying to grasp their complicated name, so loved by my Mom. Eventually making peace with herself, she started to call them Glusha. But there was a queen of flowers in our yard – it was a purple rose that was growing near the front door. It was protruding amongst all other plants with its strong stalks, sophisticated prickles, lush green leaves and amazing, heavy purple roses. Aunt Dasha was excited by this rose and couldn't choose a proper name for it, despite her rich imagination. She would just call it "our dear rose."

Apart from all its unique charm, it had another amazing trait. The rose was planted by my Mom when I was in the sixth grade and my little sister was in the third grade, and would always blossom by September 1. This traditional coincidence would repeat regularly, year after year, and my sister and I, wearing our white uniform aprons and white bowknots, carrying bunches of purple roses, were parading toward our school, distinguished by our unique flowers. Every time, when my Mom was wrapping these amazing flowers, she would say, "These flowers are so wonderful. They have their own color, shape, and vibration. They have their unique character. They are thankful and faithful. They are alive." And my sister and I would solemnly and calmly, hurry to school. Back then, we didn't understand and didn't appreciate the joy of everything happening. Time passed. My sister and I entered universities and left our parent's house. Once, coming back from the large city to my home, I felt how small and touching it was. And the flowerbed with my favorite flowers resembled the past. Despite the habitual buzzing of bees and flies, the amazing colours and combination of smells, I perceived everything in a different way. It all seemed to be a bit tiresome and less bright than it had been in the bygone days.

Even the purple rose became shorter over the years of our studies and small rose buds couldn't blossom, remaining half-open, markedly thinning as the years passed. It was still taking its centre place and my Mom liked to talk to it in the warm and brief autumn evenings. When some more time passed, I came back to my dear home, which keeps coming to me in my dreams, and brought my newborn son. After his birth, all schedules of my family members changed - obeying the single beloved being that came into this world and filled our lives.

We were putting the child to sleep in a red baby carrier, under a large nut tree that was keeping him safe from flies and bees, next to our favorite flower bed. Every evening, in accordance with tradition, we would bathe our child in lovage, inlayed on the bottom of a small enameled bath. We would swill his little body - using his Grandma's pitcher, adorned with ornaments of pansies - with flows of warmed spring water. I would always hold my son's head and my Mom (a pediatrician who had worked with children for her whole life) was bathing him with skill and love, remembering all the rules. This would always take place in the living room and was the most significant event in the house, and in the whole world.

My Grandma, who lived with us back then, instructed us to pour the water used in the baby's bathing onto the flowers before the sunset. I would pour this water on the bush of our old, beloved rose. Sometimes, we don't realise that even the most habitual things and events can encompass the essential moments of our, often inimitable, happiness. These matchless and unforgettable days were so complicated, busy, and full of problems and worries. In these days, the feelings of happiness and warmth of people united by the birth of a new person were special. I now recall this complicated time like the dearest days filled with sun and joy. By the end of the summer, we noticed the amazing transformation of our sleeping purple rose: it became stronger, gained new energy and was ready for a rematch. Its twigs spread out and gathered the former strength; its leaves became lush and bright. With new energy its prickles straightened up and a multitude of newly emerged tight buds showed translucent small holes with edges of purple petals. In the beginning of September, the rose started blossoming with a new, triumphal force. It was a miracle, an unforgettable moment. My Mom snipped the first flowers and put them in a cut-glass vase next to the baby crib. And even though, in view of her professionalism, our Mom never recommended us to put flowers in the baby's room, this time, she made an exception and said, "This rose is also our family."

Many years passed and during this time I received the most different, amazing, and even exotic flowers, sometimes collected by professional artists and florists and brought from afar. However, these roses from my childhood, with their ruthless prickles and faithful heads, remain the most beautiful and joyful flowers of my life. There was another unforgettable moment, when I saw my rose of September again. It came to me in a dream. It happened exactly on the night when my Mom died.

In my dream, it was bright, with multicoloured petals. Afterwards, involuntary marking the time when my Mom passed, I realised that it coincided with the appearance of the rose of September in my dream. She was saying goodbye to me…

"Miracle Is Where You Are..."

Several months of war destroyed the life of each person - opening an unknown page of destiny, filled with despair, separation, fear, anxieties, and irretrievable losses. Suffering and grief came into every family. Only seniors, women, and children, were left in the village that was coming closer and closer to the front. It was impossible to get used to the rumblings of cannonades, distant whistling of projectiles, and lightning blazing across the sky. The heart was wrung with the thought that soon, something horrible, irrevocable and unavoidable could happen. No one could hide or run away from it. There was a small house in the village's outskirts. It was visible due to its white color among other dwellings that stood nearby. No matter the weather, or season, the house looked attractive, impressing with its calmness., It was autumn. A cold, damp, and rainy autumn. Pain and despair dissolved in the air, in extremely cold water flows that were sinking in the dirt, and in trampling village tracks, beaten more than ever. A door opened with a creak and a house owner, Maria appeared on the threshold with her neighbour Nadya. Even though Maria had only recently turned 40, she looked older than her worldly-wise and grey-haired neighbour. Several weeks before, she had overcome a shock that coincided with the appearance of a postman who brought a ghastly envelope to her house. Half a year ago, she was helping her husband prepare to go to the darned war that took him from her so quickly and mercilessly. It took away everything: her world, her happiness, her love. They had lived together for 19 years and it was like a single moment – such a short and happy moment. Somewhere in her subconsciousness, when she would lose the sense of reality, she could convince herself that it was all a lie, a mistake. She wanted so much to change everything and return her beloved dear man at any cost. At least for a minute.

Standing in the doorway, Maria looked thinned down, haggard, with dim hollow eyes that had lost their colour because of tears. Barely audible words were coming from her dried and chapped lips. A curl of grey hair showed from under her black shawl. Her thin, bony arms were hanging along her body. Grief was standing behind this woman. It entered each cell of her soul. And there was no limit to her despair in the world, where Stepan left her - being so foolishly caught by a bullet. And their house had immediately become empty.

She was so happy in this house, where she was born. The house, where she and Stepan came to live after their wedding and where their beloved daughter came to the world. They called their baby Valentina, after his mother. This was a rare name in their village and it was given to a special girl, whom everyone called "Bell". And her parents, in their turn, were called "Newlyweds". Everyone knew Bell in the village. Every person noticed the fair-haired nimble girl who was delightfully murmuring the expressions only she could understand. Her dark-blonde hair was shining like a halo in the sun. Her blue eyes, flashing with sparks, were gazing with amazement at each passer-by. Her lips, with an attractive smile, proved her openness. Seeing Valentina, the villagers liked to say that she was the child of love.

"A miracle has to happen with her," they would say . Miracle was everywhere in this family. In every day, every minute, every event, even the simplest one. Maria was proud of Stepan and was happy to see the dimples on her daughter's cheeks that resembled those of her husband. She noted that her blue eyes that were changing colour in the light, were shining in the same manner as those of her beloved Stepan. And only the fair ashy hair in the unruly mop on her daughter's head, that was often coming out of the braid, was hers. Sometimes, she imagined it would be good if Valentina had Stepan's dark silky wavy hair that was always gliding under her fingers.

Everyone loved Valentina. Becoming older, her character changed: childish openness gave place to her restrained affection and sincere lovingness. She turned into a beautiful, slim girl that was still shining. Her hair became a bit darker and she was always braiding it, tying it with a blue, satin ribbon. Everything about this girl caught everyone's attention. Her ringing voice, the flush on her cheeks. Her disarming trust of people that revealed itself in her childish and open smile. Besides, she had a voice that didn't resemble any other. When Valentina was singing, everyone would freeze for a moment, grasping the dimensions of a completely other world.

Bell became the pride of the entire village. All over the neighborhood, everyone knew Valentina. She even went to a singing contest on the eve of the war and it was impossible not to notice her talent there. But it all seemed to happen in the previous life. War took Stepan away, filled their house with unhappiness and devastated Maria's soul. Once again, Nadya came to her neighbour, who was desperate with grief, to support her. On their hard path of this life, all villagers would do it for each other.

"Maria, you have to do something with Valentina. The Germans will soon come here. I'm telling this to you for a hundredth time and you don't react. You can't hide her. The best thing that can happen is that they will take her to Germany. People say that they do many horrible things." Maria was listening to her, aloof. She didn't have enough energy to even imagine what may follow these horrible times. But the fear for her beloved girl, who was the only person who tied her to this world, did its part. She came back to reality and looked at her neighbour.

"What should I do, Nadya?"

"You have to marry Valentina off. She will have a lawful husband who will become her first man and will protect her."

"What are you saying?! Our grief is endless."

Nadya had told her many times that in a neighbouring village, where her sister lived, military men were standing. She saw a very handsome soldier there, who even looked like Stepan.

"The guy is going to war, and who knows what trouble he will get into. You have to protect Valentina with married life."

"Nadya, what are you talking about?" Maria cried.

"We will marry them in church and the power of our common prayer will help them!" her neighbour pronounced, effusively.

Even though Nadya's suggestion was strange, Maria's intuition told her that she had to do it. But how? And how would she explain this to her daughter? And how will this soldier they don't even know react to their strange and unexpected suggestion? And where is he, this soldier? Maria came into her house. Wrapped in a shawl, Valentina was sitting on her bed. After her father's death, it was her usual pose. She had thinned down and her long, slender fingers that were holding her sharp knees, froze. Resembling a snail in this posture, she couldn't take her eyes away from the logs crackling in the stove.

"Valentina, my dear daughter. My lovely Bell. I want to talk to you. The Germans will soon come here. We have to marry you, so you will be with your husband, under protection."

"Mommy, what are you talking about?" the girl replied, fearfully. "What marriage? I want to marry someone I will love to live with, like you lived with Dad. Besides, I've never even kissed a guy before."

"This is the point, my girl. You have to marry to save yourself."

Valentina burst into tears. It seemed to her that her mother was delirious because of her grief. She felt sorry for her dear mother so much that a new wave of despair filled her soul even more, and her tears burst out. What can one change in this endless flow of human suffering? How can one hide from the war if it is in action? If one lives in the place where everything is soaked in it. Where people have no strength to think about something kind and natural in this ocean of despair and suffering.

There are moments in life, when you can actually feel the plunger that makes you act and realise that the events have their meanings on this part of your life path. You have to commit this action immediately, in a single moment. You get an impression that you've jumped into a streaming time flow of events that have been planned from above and subdued all your life to its rules. It's important to listen to what is happening and avoid resistance to your destiny.

Night was falling. Nadya came back to her house, put on her quilted coat and tied a checkered shawl onto her head. The kersey boots that her husband left at home when he went to war, were especially cherished by her at that time. She glided into her dear husband's shoes, that seemed to breathe with his warmth, sat down for a moment and performed the sign of the cross in front of a small icon of St. Nicholas, and went to visit her sister in a neighbouring village, to find Valentina's destiny. She had a gut feeling that it was inadmissible to postpone this decision that emerged so unexpectedly.

It wasn't a very far journey – only about 5 kilometers. Nadya was overfilled with the decisiveness to protect Valentina's life and she didn't doubt the rightness of her actions. Moving in her habitual quick pace along the path she had known from her childhood, Nadya let herself relive her memories. Once again, she came back to the day when the local priest, Father John, married her to her dear Sergey in the church. He said to them that from then onwards, they would be "under double protection." She could always feel this protection. When after unsuccessful childbearing she felt the breath of death and survived the bleeding. When her husband, Sergey Petrovich, coming back home at night, almost died from the hands of street rowdies and, hiding from a bullet, remained safe and sound. And at that moment, with a sinking heart, she desperately hoped that her husband was covered with the angel's wing of their mutual destiny on dangerous paths of war.

It was drizzling and the track with dirty puddles remained behind her. She knocked onto the window of her sister's house. Lyuba was younger than Nadya, but at that hour and in those circumstances, one couldn't see the age difference between the sisters. In Lyuba's house, there was a smell of tobacco, wet wool and kerosene. The grey contours of a well-known room could be seen in the darkness that was lighted only by a dwindling lamp in her sister's hands.

"Nadya, what has happened? Why have you come at this hour?" Lyuba whispered with surprise.

"It's destiny, my dear Lyuba. Valentina's destiny. You know that for Sergey and I, she's like our own daughter. Where is the young soldier I saw at your house recently? The dark-haired guy?" Nadya entered the house.

"He's still here. Sleeping in the big room. They're leaving tomorrow," Lyuba answered.

"So I came in time," Nadya blurted.

The sisters woke up the young man who could be hardly discerned in the darkness. Only his shining eyes proved the guy's quick reaction. His surprise increased when Nadya told him about the reason for her arrival. However, after a short pause, unexpectedly for both women, he agreed to this strange offer.

"Maybe it is my destiny. I'm going to the front soon and I've never even kissed a girl before. They could kill me and I won't even know why I lived," he said and smiled sadly. "Take me to my promised wife, I want to marry. I swore to my granny that I would marry a girl destined to me. And now, she has arrived into my life. As my Mom would say, destiny comes when you expect it the least."

The young man's name was Peter. Nadya took him that dark night, to her native village, to the house that was bright white in the darkness. Maria calmly prepared Valentina who didn't even resist. When the girl saw the silhouette of the young man in the darkness, she gave him her almost childish hand and felt the warmth of his fingers. This, they met in the twilight of cold autumn night at the height of the war. The four of them soon got used to the unexpected decision, and to each other. They went to the small church that was standing nearby. The priest, Father John, lived in this abode that survived by some miracle. Everything was happening quickly and resembled a chain reaction that was launching the mechanisms of unexpectedly interconnecting destinies. The priest, came to the people who awoke him. He listened to Nadya's incoherent speech and quickly understood what was happening.

For his long life, after seeing and overcoming many things, he got used to perceiving every event with a special calmness, grasping the main point in everything. He invited everyone into the church, lit two candles in front of the icon, and orchestrated the sacred union of the destinies of the two young persons that were caught in the war. The wedding ceremony in the half-destroyed old village church, with silhouettes barely seen in the dim light of candles, was very special. This whirl of events, caused by the hand of the cruel war, seemed to be the rescue beyond the limits of a merciless reality. Valentina and Peter were standing next to each other in front of the grey-haired old priest, and his quiet voice resembled a message coming from another world. In the complete absurdity of these events, all attendees had a delusive hope for a possibility of a miracle that will save them in this sad world filled with troubles.

The priest asked the newlyweds to take each other's hands and memorise the warmth of their connection. It had to be so strong that it wouldn't let any troubles destroy it. And then he turned to Peter and gave him a paper icon with the face of St. Nicholas the Wonderworker.

"He will save your family, you, and your wife from the hardships on all paths of the war. May the Guardian Angel take you back to your wife safe and sound."

And then he blessed the newlyweds.

Valentina felt his strong callous hand that carefully took her almost childish fingers. Despite the sense of unreality, it became like a message from an unknown world that gave her a new strength on the edge of grief and despair.

The darkest night comes before the dawn.

Valentina and Peter came to her house. They didn't know each other, hadn't gotten used to each other's names yet, but they already sensed the warmth when they were together. He hugged her and could smell the scent of her ashy hair that resembled the smell of apples from his garden that was so far away from here. This hour of their life was one of the greatest gifts. It took away their loneliness and grief by an unexpected will of fortune. They dissolved in this world, taking the power from the huge endless hope that saved them on the brink of an abyss.

Peter left Valentina's house with the first greyish rays of sunrise. There was an impression that the sky was lifting the curtain above the new life of these two people. Valentina frequently recalled this breaking damp sunrise, when her husband was leaving for the war. She knew only a few things about him: his name was Peter Babich, he was from Chernigov, he was 19 and he had callous hands. She knew that he would write to her, his wife, and remember her forever. She didn't remember his face. Only the touch of his hands and his close breath. And his dear and beloved silhouette that dissolved in the sunrise haze.

In a week, occupiers came to the village. Even though they were enemies, they were Romanian military men. Unlike the neighbouring villages, where Germans were raging, in their village there was no pillage, no searching for families of communists and Jews, no shootings and no violence. Maria, who lived with Valentina in the outskirts of the village, tried not to let her daughter go out in the public. Nadya shared every piece of bread and each potato with her and often brought bundles of twigs from the nearby forest. The winter was coming to an end, when Maria fell ill. In the darkness of a cold night, in her slight delirium, she heard Valentina's ringing voice, saying:

"Mommy, dear, hold on. It's so important to me. We're going to have a baby."

***

Swallows were flying in the translucent April sky, looking for places to create their homes. They chose a corner under the roof of Maria's house near Valentina's window. These miraculous birds didn't care about the sounds of shots or the chaos of soldiers running in the village. These amazing sky dwellers were living by their unchangeable laws of creation and protection of the family. Valentina was sitting on the low porch and watching the fluttering, singing birds. Closing her eyes, she inhaled the forgotten smell of the spring. It seemed to her that it had been an eternity. She became estranged from simple human joys that suddenly woke up in her soul that morning. She wanted to clean up in the house, fill it with the smell of flowers and freshly baked bread. She wanted to sing and she even tried to make some sound. But it broke... Once again, she recalled Peter and her thoughts took her to the amazing night in her life.

Her figure changed and it was especially touching to see the careful gait of the pregnant woman with hands protecting her visible belly. The cold winter, filled with fear, hunger, and endless worries, remained behind them. In her whole life before Peter, there wasn't so much grief, despair and... infinite hope at the same time. Letters didn't come to the occupied territories and Valentina invented her own alternative. She sent letters to herself, signing them "Yours, Peter" and read them in the long evenings.

In the first days of wartime summer, Valentina, the Bell, gave birth to a girl. She was also a Bell, just like herself, only, with dark hair. And the three women, who took part in creating this miracle, were crying out of happiness. Nadya took a large bowl, where they bathed the girl and later baptized her, calling her Sveta.

Father John died in that cold winter. Villagers found him lying on the floor near a half-destroyed sanctuary and buried him according to the Christian laws. But beforehand he managed to teach Nadya to baptize those who were coming to this world, as well as those who were leaving it.

And Nadya understood the importance of this mission. After some time, the village became free from occupation and gradually, life started coming back into the wounded souls and emptied houses. Valentina, Maria, and Nadya plunged into the care for Sveta. And, even though they didn't have some of the simplest and necessary things for the baby, they were happy to have someone to give this care to.

During all wartime years, a cow called Mushka came into their lives. They took care of this cow, hiding and feeding her, realizing how important she was for them. Mushka was fulfilling her tasks with understanding and, even though being skinny, gave a small but priceless portion of milk for Sveta... The war was coming to an end, and a postman came to their house. He delivered something for Valentina. It was a letter from Peter – a real one. The letter from another world and another dimension. He wrote that he had been wounded near Kursk and had been lying in a hospital. Then he recovered and returned to the front. He wrote that he loved his family and missed his beloved wife. It was happiness in the endless world of loss, pain and despair.

Sveta got used to running around the yard, looking at shining tree-beetles that were falling on the ground. In her little thin body, there was endless energy and resilience, childish concentration, and active participation in everything happening around her. The girl, with widely set eyes, was attentively watching her beloved grandmother who was crossing the yard with difficulty to meet her. It was evident that this woman grew old too early and wanted to walk quicker but couldn't. She came to the porch, sat near the door and burst out sobbing, loudly. Valentina, who ran out of the house, started calming her down, not understanding the cause of her evident despair. But it turned out that those were the tears of joy. From her mother's lips, Valentina heard a hardly distinguishable word "Victory!"

In another month, Valentina received a "killed in battle" notice about Peter. The world lost its hope, color and sound. All the focus was shifted onto Sveta who was the only thread that connected her to the minutes of her unforgettable and inimitable happiness.

After some more time, hunger, universal devastation, as well as devastation of the soul filled the world. They had to survive somehow. On a family council, the women decided that they had to sell their provider, their cow, Mushka. Valentina woke up before the sunset. The skinny cow had to be taken to a market to a nearest district centre , which was 7 kilometers away. The woman set for an uneasy journey with her dear pet that had saved her family from hunger. Her heart started aching when Valentina once again recalled the figure of her dear and beloved man.

When she got to the town with Mushka, the sun was at its height. It seemed to Valentina that people from all over the neighbourhood came to the market, filling the chaotic space. There were more people who were selling something than those who wanted to buy. And no one even came to look at her dear cow. When it became warmer and the market fuss began to get quieter, Valentina saw a handsome soldier among the dispersing crowd. He was tall, stately, and had wavy dark hair. When he turned to her, her heart started aching again. 'He looks so much like Peter, my husband...' she thought. His gaze transpierced her, and because of that she felt even worse. Everything started to wake up inside of her: her despair, her hope and her pain. Valentina couldn't hold herself anymore and tears gushed from her eyes.

"Why are you crying, beauty?" the soldier asked.

"It hurts me to sell my cow," Valentina answered as if in a dream.

"Why are you selling it then, honey?"

"I have to feed my daughter." It seemed to Valentina that someone else was speaking instead of her.

The soldier looked at the apathetic Mushka with a smile, paid a good sum for the cow and became lost in the crowd. The last words he said to her were, "Don't be sad, my dear, everything will be fine soon."

Valentina came to her senses when she remained alone amongst the market fuss. Everything happened so quickly that she didn't have time to apprehend the reality of events. And, despite the rescuing financial support, her soul was filled with anguish.

On her way back, Valentina was crying and wiping the unending gushes of tears with her work-weary hands. She gave vent to herself, to her tears, her desperate soul. It seemed to be impossible to overcome as much pain and suffering as they did during the war time. And only after she noticed the white walls of her house, the pain started soothing and she regained control over her tears. When she entered the yard, she saw her cow Mushka, who had covered much distance throughout the day. She couldn't believe her eyes and came into the house. The soldier she had met on the market was sitting at the table, taking something out of his bag. Maria looked at her daughter with a smile. It was hard for Valentina to realise what was happening. The soldier got up and couldn't say anything for several minutes. Then his quiet words came out of his lips.

"I am Peter. I saw you and thought how much you resembled my wife."

"I am your wife forever," Valentina whispered feebly.

Peter hugged Valentina and smelt the forgotten smell of apples again. Sveta was looking at them with interest from behind the curtain. Valentina took her in her arms and gave her to Peter. When he put the girl to sleep, he placed the wiped-out paper icon of St. Nicholas the Wonderworker on the bedside table.

"He saved me many times, when bullets were whistling over me. When hunger was unsettling. When everyone mistakenly thought I was dead and left me on the battlefield. When I crossed the front, gathering my last forces and reached our army. I survived. We had the protection, my dear Valentina. Our Guardian Angel has two wings. The miracle married us and it will remain with us forever."

Years went by... I sat in my modern office and my companion, Galina, a beautiful young woman who became my colleague and shared my views, told me about her plans that were interesting for both of us.

After the first minutes of our meeting, her eyes, shining like ripe cherries, drew my attention. Her face, with beautiful refined skin would cover with touching flush at each emotional outbreak. The fragrance that could be smelt in her presence resembled the smell of ripe home-grown apples.

In communication with this young woman, I made sure, once again, that people who speak in one language quickly learn to understand and feel each other. From the first moments, possibilities of limitless and trustful communication open up. For this reason, I immediately wanted to learn the source of this woman's incredible charm. After hearing my question, she looked at me, attentively, smiled and replied, "It's not accidental. I'm the envoy of love..."

That's when I learnt the amazing story of Galina's grandparents, who lived a dignified and happy life filled with love. Peter returned from the war being the Hero of the Soviet Union. He was a respectable family man. He and Valentina were called "newlyweds" till their last days. At the elderly age of 92 years old, he still looked at his Valentina, the Bell, with enamored eyes, and always said he loved her. All the time. She outlived him by one year, and passed away to meet him with a smile. This smile reflected the happiness of their endless love.

Sveta grew up, became a teacher and also married for love. Her husband saw her in a dream when he was a young man. St. Nicholas the Wonderworker blessed their meeting. Galina also has her own love story. And there is no end to that, because miracle is there for us forever! You just have to believe in it and your faith shall be rewarded…